JO

By

Julian Trinidad Gardea

Inspired by the Japanese Mythical Creature / Yokai:
JOROGUMO

EXT. WOODS - DAY

                                                    FADE IN:

Early in the morning and deep in the woods, spiders of all
shapes and sizes surge the area on land, rock and tree. A
large and strange cocoon covered in thick webbing hangs high
in the branches. As these spiders slowly make their way
across the sticky web, a gargling noise is heard from within
and the cocoon moves.

                                                   BLACK OUT:

TITLE OVER BLACKOUT WITH A FAST TEMPO OF CREEPY VIOLIN
MUSIC: "JO"

INT. JO'S APARTMENT - DAY

                                                    FADE IN:

The apartment is plain, simple and lacking of vibrancy and
personality. The space is decorated with simple furniture
and the atmosphere has no life or excitement.

BEDROOM

Alarm clock turns ON at 5:30 a.m.

JO, a slightly chubby and plain Japanese-American violinist,
introvert, in her 20's and obviously a single virgin, wakes
up. She slowly reaches out to turn OFF the loud alarm. She
yawns and begins her morning routine.

BATHROOM

Jo starts her morning by sitting on the toilet, then
showering and finally brushing her teeth while looking
depressed at her reflection. She knows her day is not going
to be different or better.

BEDROOM

Jo, wrapped in a towel, dries and brushes her hair as she
sits on her bed with a brush and blow dryer.

Walking out of her closet, she carries her outfit for the
day and throws it on the bed. A plain, black, long sleeve
blouse and a long, black skirt. Standing in front of a
mirror, she reaches out for her round frame glasses. Putting
them on, she studies her reflection and huffs in
disappointment.

KITCHEN

Jo makes herself breakfast as she hears a dog bark outside and police sirens pass by. She adds jelly to her toast and fills her cup with coffee. Sitting quietly at her table, she skims through an old fashion magazine looking at all the pretty models as she takes a crunchy bite of her bleak breakfast. Soon after, she cleans her mess up and washes the dishes.

LIVING ROOM

Jo puts on her jacket, grabs her violin case, her music folder and her purse. She then leaves the apartment.

3   **INT. CITY BUS - DAY**   3

As Jo rides the bus quietly, few of the odd looking locals on board keep to themselves, slowly trying to wake up. Jo stares out the window as traffic passes by.

4   **EXT. DOWNTOWN PERFORMANCE THEATER - DAY**   4

Jo heads towards a large building of abstract architecture with numerous trees in the area. Few people in coats walk towards the entrance with their instrument cases in one hand and a cup of coffee or a cigarette in the other.

Jo walks up the steps towards the lobby of the music hall and enters.

5   **INT. PERFORMANCE THEATER, STAGE - DAY**   5

Jo and dozens of musicians make their way to their seats with instruments in hand, preparing for their rehearsal. DR. PIETRO NICOLS, a tall, semi-handsome 50's Caucasian maestro with a pot belly walks up the stage towards his podium and music stand.

                    DR. NICOLS
          Good morning everyone.

                    ALL MUSICIANS
          Morning / Good Morning.

Dr. Nicols grabs his baton and taps it a few times on his stand. The orchestra quiets down as he raises his hands. Dr. Nicols begins to move his baton and suddenly the orchestra plays an intense and thematic opening.

Minutes through the piece, Jo begins to become distracted by first chair violinist, BONNY. Bonny is a thin, pretty Caucasian, blonde, 20's and privileged. She is always seen with her gold necklace of a Treble Clef charm.

As the orchestra plays, Bonny rises from her seat and steps away to begin playing her intricate but intense solo.

Jo suddenly makes a mistake.

Dr. Nicols flinches at the sound and stops the rehearsal.

>   DR. NICOLS
>   Stop - stop - stop! Jo - do we have
>   a problem?

>   JO
>   Um, no. Sorry!

>   DR. NICOLS
>   Just - be quiet. From the top
>   everyone!

Bonny returns to her seat with a mean look at Jo.

>   DR. NICOLS (CONT'D)
>   One, two, three...

Dr. Nicols moves his hands and the orchestra plays again.

6   **INT. PERFORMANCE THEATER, WOMEN'S BATHROOM - DAY**   6

Jo sits in a stall, quietly in tears.

>   JO
>   *(Whispers to herself)*
>   Stupid!

Bonny and her friend, FRANKIE, a pretty 20's African American flutist with short hair and spunky personality enters the bathroom laughing. As they set their belongings on the sink, they begin to touch up on their makeup and hair.

>   FRANKIE
>   Why does Nicols keep her around?
>   She is not that good!

>   BONNY
>   I don't get it either!

>   FRANKIE
>   Did you see how she keeps looking
>   at you?

>   BONNY
>   Ugh, fucking rug muncher. I get the
>   creeps if I even *feel* like she's
>   watching me.

                          FRANKIE
              She should've just played the
              French Horn. At least she has her
              hand in a hole other than herself.

Bonny and Frankie laugh as they leave the bathroom.

                          BONNY
              What a loser!

Jo wipes away her tears and leaves the stall. She stares
into a mirror for a moment and suddenly hears the door open.
She quickly leaves the bathroom as she bumps into a small
group of FEMALE MUSICIANS walking in.

                          FEMALE WOMAN
              What's her problem?

7   **INT. PERFORMANCE THEATER, STAGE - DAY**   7

Coming to a close of a musical number, Dr. Nicols wafts his
hands and the music stops.

                          DR. NICOLS
              Good job, everyone. See you all
              tomorrow!

The musicians begin to dissipate across the stage.

8   **INT. PERFORMANCE THEATER, BACKSTAGE - DAY**   8

Backstage is lightly lit, showing a scene of ropes, pulleys,
props and other equipment.

As Jo puts her violin away, Dr. Nicols comes up behind her.

                          DR. NICOLS
              Jo.

                          JO
              Yes. Dr. Nicols, I am so...

                          DR. NICOLS
              Come. Let's talk in my office.

Bonny and Frankie notice Dr. Nicols leading Jo towards his
office. The women EXIT in laughter as they leave backstage.

INT. DR. NICOLS' OFFICE - DAY

As Dr. Nicols enters his office, the room is decorated with mid-century furniture and minimalist art.

> DR. NICOLS
> Get your violin out.

As she follows his instruction, she watches him pull out a music stand for her. He then walks around his desk to take a seat. Jo stands there silent.

> DR. NICOLS (CONT'D)
> Well?

> JO
> Um, what do you want me to play?

> DR. NICOLS
> What the hell do you think? The show, Jo! The fucking show! Start from the beginning!

> JO
> Sorry, yes.

> DR. NICOLS
> Stop saying 'sorry'. Better yet, just stop talking and get your music out, now.

Opening up her folder on the stand, she waits for a moment and starts playing.

After a short while, Dr. Nicols stands from his desk, walks towards her and removes the music sheets from her sight.

Jo stops.

> DR. NICOLS (CONT'D)
> Keep playing! In fact, I want you to play Bonny's solo.

Jo hesitates but nervously starts playing the solo. After a moment, he wafts his hands at her to stop.

> DR. NICOLS (CONT'D)
> I don't understand. Beautiful. Just beautiful. You even memorized it. So what's the problem?

              JO
I don't know.

           DR. NICOLS
Yes, you do. Bonny.

              JO
What?

           DR. NICOLS
You keep looking at Bonny?

              JO
No, I don't.

           DR. NICOLS
I see everything. Jo, I don't care
if you're a lesbian. But I need you
to pay attention during rehearsal.

              JO
But I am not, a lesbian.

           DR. NICOLS
       (He begins to circle around Jo
       like a hungry vulture.)
So why do you keep staring at her?
Oh, is it because she's first
chair? You know, mistakes is not
going to make you move up from
second. Do you even like playing
with us, Jo?

              JO
Yes.

           DR. NICOLS
       (Stops behind Jo and observes
       her body)
If you want to be the best. Become
better than Bonny, you are going to
have to push yourself closer to the
edge. You play with hallow
calculation instead of with emotion
and passion.

Dr. Nicols slowly raises his hands to hover over Jo's
shoulders.

         DR. NICOLS (CONT'D)
       (Slowly grasps onto Jo's
       shoulders)
Do you want to be the best, Jo? To
perform with raw feelings where the
           (MORE)

> DR. NICOLS (CONT'D)
> audience just wants to hear more of
> you? To *see* more of you?

> JO
> *(Nervously shaking)*
> Yes.

> DR. NICOLS
> *(Leans into whisper in her*
> *ear)*
> What would you be willing to do,
> for that moment?

> JO
> What do you mean?

Dr. Nicols begins to breathe heavily as if he is inhaling
her smell and then chuckles. Walking past her, he moves
towards his desk.

> DR. NICOLS
> Go home, Jo. You have the talent
> but no heart. Playing music should
> be like making love and you sound
> like the hollow and an emotionless
> soundtrack of a porno.

Jo suddenly becomes shocked and angry.

> DR. NICOLS (CONT'D)
> No mistakes tomorrow. Do you
> understand?

> JO
> Yes.

> DR. NICOLS
> You can go.

Jo quickly puts her violin back in her case. As she reaches
for her folder, she accidentally knocks over the music
stand. Grabbing fistful of her music sheets from the floor,
she quickly flees from the office.

Dr. Nicols slowly walks to his desk and sits on the edge.
Pondering in dirty thoughts.

10   **INT. PERFORMANCE THEATER, HALLWAY - DAY**   10

Jo quickly runs down an empty hallway as her shoes echo loudly.

11   **EXT. DOWNTOWN PERFORMANCE THEATER - DAY**   11

Jo exits from the building in tears.

As she stops several yards from the building, she stops and cries.

12   **INT. CITY BUS - DAY**   12

Jo rides the bus back home with puffy cheeks and red eyes. Just like before, she stares out the window observing the afternoon traffic.

13   **INT. JO'S APARTMENT - NIGHT**   13

KITCHEN

Jo picks at her bowl of macaroni and cheese. Her glass of milk remains untouched.

BATHROOM

Jo stares at herself in the mirror. Unhappy with what she sees, she looks under her sink and digs around. She pulls out an old, dusty, black cosmetic bag. Searching in the bag, she pulls out a variety of makeup items. Jo opens up a tube of bright, red lipstick.

Lying in a tub filled with soapy water, Jo's face is dolled up with poor result and technique. She listens quietly as droplets from the faucet hit the water.

Closing her eyes to meditate, she is unaware that a brown spider is crawling across her shower rod.

Jo begins to wash her face.

LIVING ROOM

In a over sized white t-shirt, she stands with her violin and begins to practice.

                                                          FADE OUT

14   **INT. JO'S APARTMENT - DAY**   14

Alarm clock turns ON at 5:30 a.m.

15   **INT. CITY BUS - DAY**   15

Jo rides the bus and stares at traffic.

16   **INT. MUSIC HALL STAGE - DAY**   16

The orchestra is in the middle of playing an intense piece.
As Jo is dressed in plain, black clothes, she finds herself
staring at Dr. Nicols.

Dr. Nicols rigorously moves his arms as the music comes to a
dramatic close.

The orchestra sits silently.

                    DR. NICOLS
          Perfect! That's how I want you all
          to play, every time! You guys sound
          fucking amazing!

The musicians laugh and applause. As Dr. Nicols continue
talking, she takes notice of his hands, lips and eyes.

                    DR. NICOLS (CONT'D)
          Concert is this Saturday. Everyone
          can go home early today. Final
          rehearsal is tomorrow!

The musicians celebrate. As they leave their seats, Jo
watches Dr. Nicols EXIT backstage.

17   **INT. PERFORMANCE THEATER, WOMEN'S BATHROOM - DAY**   17

Jo walks in the bathroom and listens carefully. She quickly
walks pass each stall while pushing on every door to make
sure that each unit is empty.

Stopping at the end, she quickly places her stuff down and
pulls out the cosmetic bag from her purse. Digging through,
she pulls out mascara.

Jo takes a quick moment to look at her reflection and then
attempts at the first stroke on her eye lashes. She quickly
fails at the third stroke and pokes her right eye.

                    JO
               (As she drops the brush into
               the sink)
          Ouch!

As Jo reaches for the brush with her right hand, something quickly touches her fingers from the drain. A creepy, hairy, black spider!

Jo gives out a quick SCREAM.

The spider's legs quickly disappear into the drain as she rubs her hands in horror. She dashes towards the sink and turns on the faucet, attempting to flush the creature down.

Jo quickly moves onto the next sink to wash her hands and then her sore right eye.

Door opens and in ENTERS Frankie.

                    FRANKIE
               (Smiling devilishly)
          What are you doing here, Jo?

                    JO
          Sorry, nothing.

                    FRANKIE
          Oh, I see more than nothing. That's
          for sure.
               (Chuckles)
          Are you putting on makeup?

Jo remains silent.

                    FRANKIE (CONT'D)
               (Places her flute case and
               purse down.)
          I didn't know you wear makeup.
          What's the occasion? Is it your
          birthday or something?

                    JO
          No.

                    FRANKIE
               (Studies Jo)
          Ah, it's for a girl!

                    JO
          No!

                    FRANKIE
          Hmmm. Well who is the lucky guy
          then? Tell me!

                    JO
          (Frantically puts away the
          makeup)
    It's for no one.

               FRANKIE
    Oh, don't be like that! You can
    tell me.

Jo grabs her things and starts making her way towards the
door.

            FRANKIE (CONT'D)
    I can teach you how to put on
    make-up! If you're interested.

Jo stops and thinks for a moment.

            FRANKIE (CONT'D)
    Come on back! Let's be girlfriends!

Jo turns around and walks back.

Jo finds herself leaning against a sink as Frankie is in the
middle of working on her face.

            FRANKIE (CONT'D)
    It's Eddie, right?

               JO
    Huh?

               FRANKIE
    Eddie, the bassoonist. He's the
    guy, right? He is cute.

               JO
    No.

               FRANKIE
    Kyle?

Jo shakes her head.

            FRANKIE (CONT'D)
         (As she applies the lipstick)
    Stevenson? Javier? Brandon? Oh, I
    know now... it's Dr. Nicols, isn't?

Jo looks away in embarrassment.

                    FRANKIE (CONT'D)
               (Laughs)
          Oh don't worry sweetie, I am not
          going to tell anyone. He's kind of
          hot. I'd hit it.

Jo looks at her in worry.

                    JO
          Promise you won't tell?

                    FRANKIE
               (Crosses her heart)
          Cross my heart!

                    JO
          Honestly, I don't know if I like
          him. I don't know why I am doing
          this, actually.

                    FRANKIE
               (Continues on with the makeup)
          Does he like you?

                    JO
          I think so. Where's Bonny?

                    FRANKIE
          Oh, she's... in a meeting with Dr.
          Nicols. And done!

Jo smiles and turns around in nervousness. As she stares at
herself, she is impressed.

                    FRANKIE (CONT'D)
          You know, your makeup set is old as
          shit. But I must say, I am an
          artist!

                    JO
          Do you think he will like me like
          this?

                    FRANKIE
               (Smiles devilishly)
          Oh, yeah! He'll like you?

                    JO
               (Smiles wide)
          Thank you! Could you do my makeup
          on Saturday, you know... for the
          show?

> FRANKIE
> For sure! Well, I gotta go hot
> stuff!

> JO
> Okay.

Frankie grabs her stuff, heads towards the door and opens it.

> JO (CONT'D)
> Frankie. Thanks.

Frankie smiles and leaves.

18   **INT. PERFORMANCE THEATER, HALLWAY - DAY**   18

Frankie walks away from the bathroom and pulls out her phone. She starts dialing for Bonny.

19   **INT. DR. NICOLS' OFFICE - DAY**   19

Bonny's cellphone RINGS.

Sounds of intercourse between Bonny and Dr. Nicols is heard in the background.

INTERCUT BETWEEN FRANKIE AND DR. NICOLS' OFFICE

Frankie hears Bonny's voicemail.

> BONNY (VOICE MAIL)
> Hey, you reached Bonny! You know
> what to do!

A beep is heard.

> FRANKIE
> It's Frankie. You're not going to
> believe who I ran into in the
> bathroom? Call me when you get
> this!

Bonny's phone rings with a notification of a new voice mail. Blurred in the background, Dr. Nicols arches his back as he comes to an orgasm.

> DR. NICOLS
> Oh, my darling. My little,
> beautiful talent!

20 **EXT. DOWNTOWN PERFORMANCE THEATER - DAY** 20

Jo walks out with a smile and a boost of confidence.

21 **INT. JO'S APARTMENT COMPLEX, HALLWAY - DAY** 21

As Jo climbs the stairs, she notices a girl carrying a box
in front of her.

RANI SALUJA, a young, hip, late 20's Indian American girl
with doe eyes and long, brown hair in a ponytail, drops the
box. The box flings open and bursts open with various books
on forensic medicine.

                    RANI
          Shit!

                    JO
          Oh no!

As the girls pick the books up from the steps, Jo notices
the subject matter.

                    RANI
          Thank you so much! I am new here!

                    JO
          Welcome!

                    RANI
          Thanks! I'm Rani.

The girls shake hands.

                    JO
          I'm Jo, nice to meet you. Are you a
          medical student?

                    RANI
          Doctor, well intern actually. I'll
          be one of the Medical Examiners
          downtown. As you can probably tell
          from my books. What about you?

                    JO
          I graduated this past spring. I got
          my Masters in music.

                    RANI
               (Looks at Jo's music case)
          Cool! The violin?

> JO
>
> Yes!

> RANI
>
> It's my favorite instrument. My
> aunt plays it as well.

> JO
>
> Professionally?

> RANI
>
> She used to back home, not anymore.
> Family got in the way. You know how
> the story goes.

> JO
>
> Can I help with your boxes.

> RANI
>
> That would be awesome. But this, is
> literally the last box. Come on up,
> you can join me for celebratory
> drink.

> JO
> (Smiles)
> Um... okay.

As they walk together, they stop at Rani's door and to Jo's
surprise it is directly across from her apartment.

> JO
>
> Oh, wow. You live right across from
> me.

> RANI
>
> Really? Cool! Can you get the door?

> JO
>
> Oh, sorry.

> RANI
> (Laughs)
> It's cool, thanks!

22   **INT. RANI'S APARTMENT - DAY**   22

LIVING ROOM

As Jo and Rani ENTER, Jo notices the various stacked boxes
around the apartment. Rani places the box on her small
dining table and moves towards the kitchen.

> RANI
> You can put your stuff down, relax.

Jo does as she requested.

KITCHEN

Rani opens the fridge and pulls out two bottled beers and twists off the cap.

> RANI (CONT'D)
> *(Passing a bottle to Jo)*
> So how long have you lived here?

> JO
> *(Looking around the area)*
> Two years.

> RANI
> *(Taking a quick swig of her beer)*
> And, how do you like it?

> JO
> I like it. It's quiet. It's an okay neighborhood.

> RANI
> Cool. Any cute boys that live here?

> JO
> Oh, um.

> RANI
> *(Laughs)*
> No pressure!

> JO
> *(Smiles lightly)*
> I don't know.

> RANI
> Well, we're going to have to find them ourselves - aren't we?

> JO
> I have to go.

> RANI
> No, you don't have to. Actually, I'll tell you what! Since I just moved in and I'm your new neighbor! Let's go out tonight!

                    JO
          Uh, no. I - I have rehearsal
          tomorrow morning.

                    RANI
          Oh, girl! We're not going to get
          shit faced! A few drinks, some
          laughs. You know, what friends do.

Jo contains her excitement on learning of her new found
friendship.

                    RANI (CONT'D)
          So... what do you say?

                    JO
          Okay. But not too late. I do have
          rehearsal...

                    RANI
               (Quickly downs her beer)
          Yes, tomorrow morning, I remember!
          No worries. I'll knock on your door
          around 6! Drinks and then dinner,
          okay?

                    JO
          Okay. Six.

Jo places her beer down on the table.

LIVING ROOM

Jo collects her things and makes her way to the door.

                    JO (CONT'D)
               (Exits the apartment)
          Bye.

KITCHEN

                    RANI
          See ya.

Rani notices Jo's beer bottle is still full.

                    RANI (CONT'D)
          God, I hope she's not a complete
          weirdo.

Rani starts drinking from Jo's bottle.

23   **INT. JO'S APARTMENT - DAY**   23

LIVING ROOM

Jo's cell phone RINGS as she enters her apartment. Putting her case on the couch, she reaches into her purse and pulls out her ringing phone.

Screen on phone reads MOM.

Jo accepts the call.

                 JO
         Hello. Mom?

JO'S MOM, is a 50's Caucasian woman, with a minor Texas accent.

                 JO'S MOM (V.O.)
         Hello sweetie! How are you?

24   **INT. JO'S PARENTS' HOME - DAY**   24

Jo's parents' home is bright and colorful with West Texas style furnishings.

KITCHEN

Jo's mom is on her Bluetooth earpiece as she is cutting vegetables.

INTERCUT between Jo and Jo's Mom.

                 JO
             (Sits on couch)
         I'm fine. How about you?

                 JO'S MOM
         I'm wonderful. Your dad bought
         another horse the other day!

                 JO
         Really?

                 JO'S MOM
         He sure did! You know, I didn't
         think you'd pick up when I called.
         I thought you would be at practice
         or something.

                 JO
         I was. Uh - but the director let us
         go early. You and dad are still
         flying in tomorrow right?

>   JO'S MOM
> Oh honey, that's why I am calling.
> We can't make it to your concert.

>   JO
> Is everything okay?

>   JO'S MOM
> We're fine! It just. Well, your
> grandmother fell in the shower this
> morning and broke her arm and hip.

>   JO
> Oh no! Did you want me to come
> home?

>   JO'S MOM
> No! No. You have your concert this
> weekend. And your dad is on a
> flight right now to Arizona to see
> her.

>   JO
> You are not going with him?

>   JO'S MOM
> No. Someone has to stay and watch
> the animals.

>   JO
> What happened to the guy you hired
> to help you on the ranch?

>   JO'S MOM
> Who? Henry? Oh darling, we had to
> fire him. Your father caught him
> abusing the animals!

>   JO
> Why would he do that?

>   JO'S MOM
> I don't know. These youngsters are
> becoming terrible! I am just glad
> and thankful for the Lord you came
> out fine. But I'm so sorry sweetie,
> we are going to have miss your
> concert.

>   JO
> It's okay, mom.

                    JO'S MOM
We haven't been able to hire
someone in time and with everything
with your grandma, it's just bad
timing right now. Again your daddy
and I are very sorry and we know
it's the last concert of the
season. But we will make it to your
next one, okay?

                    JO
Okay.

                    JO'S MOM
Oh darling, I love you so much!

                    JO
          (Sounding sad)
I love you too mom.

                    JO'S MOM
Everything okay?

                    JO
Actually, yeah. I made a friend
today.

                    JO'S MOM
Get out! Oh darling, tell me about
this boy. What's his name?

                    JO
Her name is Rani.

                    JO'S MOM
          (Sounds surprised)
Oh, it's a girl. You know after two
years of living in that city. You'd
think you would have a boyfriend by
now.

                    JO
Mom, please stop.

                    JO'S MOM
Sorry, sorry. You are right. So
tell me about this Rani girl.

                    JO
Nothing much really. She's new in
the building and we just met and
she wants to hang out for drinks
tonight.

                         JO'S MOM
          That is wonderful! I am so happy
          for you.

Smoke appears from the oven behind Jo's Mom.

                         JO'S MOM (V.O.)
          Well you have fun and be safe. Oh
          God!

                         JO
          Mom, are you okay?

Jo's Mom opens the oven door and smoke rolls out. Moments
later, the fire alarm turns ON.

                         JO'S MOM
                     (Speaks Loudly)
          I have to go sweetie, my bread is
          burning in the oven! Call me when
          you get back home tonight, okay?

                         JO
          Okay, I love you mo-

Jo's Mom hangs up.

Jo looks at her phone and then attempts to toss it onto the
seat next to her. But fails as the phone is stuck to her
right hand. As she grabs the phone with her left, she
notices a thin trail of sticky and thin residue between the
phone's back side and her fingers.

As she rubs the substance with her fingertips, she begins to
smell it. It was odorless.

She quickly gets up and heads to the kitchen.

KITCHEN

Jo turns on the faucet and washes her hands out. She
then wets a cloth and wipes down her phone.

LIVING ROOM

Collecting her stuff from the couch, she heads to her
bedroom and shuts the door.

INT. JO'S APARTMENT - NIGHT

BATHROOM

Jo turns off the shower and steps out of the tub to reach
for a towel. As the bathroom is filled with steam, Jo begins
to wipe the mirror with her hand.

Jo studies herself for a moment and then EXITS to the living
room.

Trails of moisture from the steam begins to slide down the
bathroom mirror and a portion of the wall that is being
reflected begins to slowly move. As if camouflaging the wall
paper design, a faint but very LARGE spider (only seen by
the shadows of its legs and abdomen) takes slow steps up the
wall, then stops and suddenly disappears.

LIVING ROOM

Jo walks into the living room dressed in a black culotte
pants and a grey blouse. She carries her grey flats (shoes)
in one hand and her purse in the other.

Coming around her sofa, Jo places her shoes on the floor and
takes a seat. Looking at her phone, the screen reads 5:35
p.m.

Jo sits back and looks around the room. As she rests her
head back, she stares at the ceiling and slowly closes her
eyes.

                                                    FADE OUT

                                                     FADE IN

KITCHEN

Slowly rising from the sink's drain is a spider and soon a
trail of them swarm in different directions of the kitchen.

BEDROOM

Numerous spiders start to crawl from beneath Jo's bed and
swarm the entire space (floors and walls).

LIVING ROOM

Tiny spiders begins to enter from the A/C vents and all the
spiders of the entire apartment begin to swarm towards Jo,
still sleeping on the couch. As they begin to crawl on the
couch, they slowly CREEP up her legs, arms and chest towards
her face. Behind the sofa, a very LARGE two-foot brown
spider begins to emerge and stand over Jo's head.

Suddenly, this large spider stands on it's hind legs and hisses while it exposes its large fangs, dripping of venom.

A KNOCK is heard on her door and Jo suddenly WAKES UP in terror.

Launching off from her sofa, she quickly scrapes her entire clothes and hair believing the spiders from her nightmare are still there.

The knock continues.

Jo looks around and finds no trace of any spider. As she makes her way to the door, she tries to fix her clothes and hair while looking at her entire apartment.

Opening the door, Rani stands in a casual blue dress and light coat.

>   RANI
>   Hey, you ready?

Jo looks behind her to inspect the apartment once more.

>   RANI (CONT'D)
>   Are you okay?

>   JO
>   Yeah, I am fine. I just...

>   RANI
>   What?

>   JO
>   Nothing. I just had a bad dream.
>   Let me get my shoes and purse.

>   RANI
>   Cool.

As Jo goes back to collect her things, she puts her shoes on. Rani remains by the door.

>   RANI (CONT'D)
>   I hope you like jazz. I did some
>   googling and there's this place a
>   few blocks from here that has happy
>   hour.

>   JO
>   That sounds fine.

Jo makes her way out of the apartment and shuts the door.

INT. JAZZ CLUB - NIGHT

The jazz club is a dark place with dim red and blue lighting. The waitstaff are dressed in black and wearing silk, purple ties. The patrons smile, flirt, laugh and move their heads with the beat.

Walking towards a small round table on the second level balcony, Jo and Rani are led by a HOSTESS. They take off their jackets and begin to sit down.

                    HOSTESS
              (Places down a small menu)
          Your waitress will be with you
          shortly.

                    JO AND RANI
          Thank you.

As the Hostess leaves, Rani and Jo take a moment to observe the small stage. A SAXOPHONIST plays a hot and speedy tempo as he and his small band entertain the audience.

                    RANI
          Are you a fan of Jazz?

                    JO
              (Nods and smiles)
          Uh-huh.

                    RANI
              (Smiling)
          You don't get out much, do you?

                    JO
              (feeling guilty)
          Actually, no. I don't have much
          friends, so I don't get the
          opportunities to go out often. And
          besides, I am always at rehearsals
          or practicing at home.

A WAITRESS walks up to their table.

                    WAITRESS
          Evening ladies. What can I get you
          to drink?

                    RANI
          I will take a Manhattan.

                        JO
          Just water, please.

                        RANI
          No! She needs a drink.

                        JO
          But I told you, I have rehearsal
          tomorrow.

                        RANI
          I know. But at least have one
          drink. Enjoy yourself, remember
          we're celebrating me moving in. And
          I don't want to drink alone.

                        JO
          Okay. Do you have something sweet?

                        WAITRESS
          How about an appletini?

                        JO
          I'll try that.

                        WAITRESS
          Great. I will be right back.

The Waitress leaves as Jo turns to watch the Saxophonist
continue playing something wild.

                        RANI
          So are you dating anyone?

                        JO
                   (Smiling)
          No. You?

                        RANI
          I was seeing someone. But it was
          him or my career kind of moment.
          Obviously, I chose the latter.

                        JO
          Do you miss him?

Suddenly, the Waitress appears with their drinks.

                        WAITRESS
          Okay ladies. One Manhattan and one
          appletini.

                  RANI
Nice! Thank you!

                WAITRESS
Anything to eat?

                  RANI
Drinking for now, maybe something
later.

                WAITRESS
Well then, you all enjoy.

Rani raises her glass.

                  RANI
    Cheers!

Jo grabs her drink and clinks her glass with Rani's

                  JO
    Cheers.

They each take a sip. Jo quickly squirms at the taste of the
alcohol.

                JO (CONT'D)
That is strong!

                  RANI
        (Laughs)
Well you better enjoy it.

Jo takes another sip.

                  JO
So, do you miss him?

                  RANI
Nah, he was one of those guys that
you knew was not going anywhere
with their lives. He wasn't even
going to school. Best advice, stay
away from online dating. So many
cute guys on there, but so many
lost causes they turn out to be.

Jo laughs and takes another sip.

TIME PASSES BY

Jo and Rani work on their second round of drinks as they
listen to another set on stage.

                         JO
                    (Sounds buzzed)
          I moved here from Texas on a
          scholarship and my parents freaked
          at first of me wanting to move up
          north to a big city.

                         RANI
          Small town girl, huh?

                         JO
          Pretty much, my parents own a
          ranch.

                         RANI
          Fascinating! Tell me about them.

Jo takes another sip.

                         JO
          There's not much to say. Well
          they're sweet, loving and I am
          thankful for them to have chosen
          me. I don't know where I would be
          if it weren't for them.

                         RANI
          What do you mean?

                         JO
          I was adopted.

                         RANI
          Really?

                         JO
          Yup!

                         RANI
          Do you know anything about your
          birth-parents?

                         JO
          Not at all. My parents did tell me
          that I was born in Japan and that
          the authorities found me in a
          forest wrapped in a blanket,
          abandoned at birth. And that is it.

                         RANI
          A forest. You gotta be fucking
          kidding me?

                         JO
          Nope!

                         RANI
          Well did you do any further
          research on your own?

                         JO
          Not really, though I - uh, when I
          was ten years old I was trying to
          find my cat. But instead, I found a
          folder in my dad's office.

27   **INT. JO'S PARENTS' HOME - DAY**   27

OFFICE

The office space is small with a wooden desk & chair and a
small library.

YOUNGER JO (10 years old) walks in wearing summer clothing.

                    YOUNGER JO
          Lexi. Here kitty kitty. Lexi.

Younger Jo looks around the office and stops behind the
desk. Bending down, she looks underneath and searches for
her missing cat.

                    YOUNGER JO (CONT'D)
          Lexi?

She suddenly notices a corner of a folder peeping out from
the back end of a drawer with small, handwritten Japanese
characters.

Younger Jo opens the drawer and reaches in and pulls out the
worn out folder with various characters written on it.
Opening it, she finds a manila envelope. She unravels the
string holding the fold and opens it. Pinching at the first
page, she begins to slowly pull out a large, black and white
photo.

As she notices the first portion of the photo revealing
blurred trees in the background. She then catches sight of a
glistened string and eventually a portion of a large but
destroyed spider's web.

                    YOUNGER JO'S MOM
                    (Shouts)
          Jo, what are you doing?

> YOUNGER JO
> *(Drops the folder)*
> Nothing!

Younger Jo's Mom walks towards her and quickly grabs the folder from the floor. Shoving the photo back in, Jo's Mom closes the folder and quickly drives Younger Jo away from the desk.

> YOUNGER JO'S MOM
> I told you many times to stay out of your father's office! What were you doing with this?

> YOUNGER JO
> I'm sorry, mommy!

HALLWAY

Younger Jo's Mom closes the office door.

> YOUNGER JO'S MOM
> Don't ever touch this, okay? Now go outside. Go!

Younger Jo scurries away as Younger Jo's Mom heads to her bedroom and slams the door shut.

28 **INT. JAZZ CLUB - NIGHT**   28

> JO
> After that, I never really looked into it further.

> RANI
> Why was your mom so crazy about keeping it a secret?

> JO
> I don't know, maybe she was just trying to protect me. Con-Artist dad and junkie mother? Who knows?

Jo sits for a moment, thinking about that day. Rani takes another sip as the Waitress appears again by their table.

> WAITRESS
> Another round, ladies?

> RANI
> Yes, please!

                    JO
No.

                    RANI
I am not going to keep fighting you
all night. We are relaxing, cutting
loose and having fun! She will have
one more and then we'll take the
check!

Jo smiles and nods in defeat.

                    WAITRESS
Okay.

The waitress leaves.

                    RANI
So how do you like playing violin?

                    JO
It's amazing. I love it. My parents
wanted me to be a doctor or lawyer.

                    RANI
Sounds like my parents.

                    JO
But I really love music. I always
saw myself... actually it's silly.

                    RANI
No, go ahead.

                    JO
Well, sometimes I imagine myself in
a beautiful dress just playing in
front of a large audience with an
incredible orchestra. Maybe in
Paris or somewhere exotic and far
away. Ever since I was a kid,
something told me I needed to play
something with strings.

                    RANI
So what drew you to the violin in
particular?

                    JO
Not sure. What's weird, long before
I picked up the violin I actually
had dreams of playing some strange
looking guitar in the middle of a
                  (MORE)

                    JO (CONT'D)
          dark forest. And I can see only the
          woods around me and my fingers
          plucking on strings.

                    RANI
          So why didn't you pick up the
          guitar instead?

                    JO
          My mom hated the idea, but my dad
          loved it. So I had to choose
          something they would both approve.
          But the instrument I was dreaming,
          it wasn't something I recognized.
          It had only three strings with a
          long neck. It looked foreign and
          old, like a traditional instrument.

                    RANI
          Weird.

                    JO
          Yeah.

29   **EXT. JAZZ CLUB - NIGHT**   29

        Jo and Rani leave the club laughing and start walking down
        the sidewalk.

                    RANI
          I am hungry!

                    JO
          There's a pizza joint around the
          corner.

                    RANI
          Let's do it!

        Jo and Rani laugh as they walk away, arms hooked with one
        another.

30   **INT. JO'S APARTMENT COMPLEX, HALLWAY - NIGHT**   30

        Walking to their doors, Jo and Rani laugh as they pull out
        there keys and open their own doors.

                    RANI
          Goodnight, girl!

                          JO
                      (Laughs)
                  Goodnight.

31   **INT. JO'S APARTMENT - NIGHT**   31

LIVING ROOM

Jo opens the door and walks in laughing and quickly closes
the door. Her laughs suddenly stop as she leans against the
door and meditates on the evening's events. She smiles and
chuckles.

Jo tosses her purse on the couch and kicks off her shoes.

KITCHEN

Jo pulls out a glass from her cabinet, fills it to the top
with water and drinks.

BATHROOM

Jo washes her face and brushes her teeth.

BEDROOM

Jo changes into her over sized t-shirt again.

LIVING ROOM

Jo stands with her violin and begins to practice.

BEDROOM

Jo gets into bed. As she lies on her side, she goes into a
deep thought and eventually closes her eyes.

32   **DREAM SEQUENCE - DARK SPACE**   32

Flashing strobes of white light flicker in the dark and
suddenly a HORRIFIC AND SCARY figure appears.

Standing still like a statue, its front side is covered in
shadows as the light continues to strobe behind it.

A NAKED woman with arms outstretched arches her back to show
the lining of her breasts and ribs. However, from the waist
down is that of a large spider; a hardened body and legs
with prickly hairs and spikes.

Suddenly a FLASH of its face appears, covered in white
light.

The head is that of a woman with dark, black hair wrapped in rolls similar to that of the traditional Geisha. Skin painted white and her mouth is in complete horror. From the nose to the chin, her mouth vertically expands wide open to reveal that of large spider fangs covered in blood and disfigured sharp teeth.

33   **INT. JO'S APARTMENT - DAY**   33

BEDROOM

Jo quickly WAKES from the NIGHTMARE. Grabbing her chest in fear, she quickly feels something is wrong with her. Feeling like she is about to vomit, she quickly runs to the bathroom.

BATHROOM

Turning on the light, she quickly drops to her knees in front of the toilet and vomits. Leaning against the tub, she wipes away the sweat on her forehead, while the vomit in the toilet shows a hint of blood. As she reaches for the knob, she flushes the waste away. Slowly standing up, she walks to the sink and washes her mouth.

Splashing her face with cold water, she stares at herself in the mirror. Suddenly she hears her alarm clock turn ON.

34   **INT. PERFORMANCE THEATER, STAGE - DAY**   34

In the middle of an intense rehearsal, Dr. Nicols flays his hands in the air trying to bring up a dramatic crescendo.

Jo, with bags under her eyes, struggles to play an intricate piece as she tries to stay in sync with Bonny and the rest of her section of violinist.

Bonny, with her trained ear begins to notice her delays. Dr. Nicols begins to notice it too and flinches his head. A section of the music with a break for the violins comes up and Bonny quickly looks sternly at Jo.

                    BONNY
                (Whispers harshly)
        What the fuck is wrong with you?

Jo beings to become worried as she catches sight of Dr. Nicols becoming angry at her.

The violin section quickly raises their instruments to continue playing.

Jo's struggle continues.

Dr. Nicols begins to grow angry as he listens to Jo's lagging of timing and precision. Suddenly, he tosses his baton to the side and grabs his music stand and THROWS it off the stage in FURY.

The orchestra suddenly STOPS in fear. Dr. Nicols runs his fingers through his hair and breathes deep as he has his back turned against the orchestra. Calming down, he looks at his watch.

Walking up to Jo, he leans in over her stand.

                    DR. NICOLS
          I don't know what's wrong with you
          and quite honest, I don't give a
          shit. But you got one hour to get
          it under control.

Dr. Nicols quickly turns around, marches off the stage and up the aisle of seats.

                    DR. NICOLS (CONT'D)
          Everyone go to lunch!

Dr. Nicols explodes open the theater doors and disappears into the lobby.

Jo, embarrassed can feel everyone's eyes on her as they begin to leave their seats.

                    BONNY
               (Leaning towards Jo)
          Why don't you just quit. You know,
          no matter how pretty you think you
          are or how much makeup you put on.
          Nicols would rather fuck a two
          dollar whore than go near you
          virginal muffin top.

Jo listens to Bonny's wretched comment as she watches Frankie dismantle her flute while chuckling at her. As Frankie stands, Bonny quickly joins her and they both leave towards the backstage.

35   **EXT. DOWNTOWN PERFORMANCE THEATER - DAY**   35

Jo sits on a wooden bench at a plaza, staring into nothing while deep in thought. Breathing heavily, she grips her fingers over the edge of her seat. Closing her eyes and taking a deep breath, she holds it in for a moment. She slowly exhales and stands up.

As she turns, she is surprised by Dr. Nicols standing there.

                         DR. NICOLS
              Follow me.

36   **INT. PERFORMANCE THEATER, HALLWAY - DAY**   36

      Jo follows closely behind Dr. Nicols as both their steps
      echo in the hallway.

37   **INT. DR. NICOLS' OFFICE - DAY**   37

      Dr. Nicols opens the door and marches towards a file cabinet
      behind his desk. Jo slowly walks into the office.

                         DR. NICOLS
                    (Pulls open a drawer and
                    searches within)
              Get in and shut the door and sit
              down.

      Jo closes the door slowly and suddenly hears a cabinet
      drawer SLAM shut.

      Jo quickly turns around as she watches Dr. Nicols turn
      around with a bottle of whiskey and an empty glass.

                         DR. NICOLS (CONT'D)
                    (Places his glass on the table
                    and starts pouring)
              Are you trying to fuck with me and
              my show?

                         JO
                    (Walks towards the chair and
                    sits)
              No. I am just not feeling well.

                         DR. NICOLS
              Do you have any idea how important
              this show is to me? Do you?

      Jo sits there silent as he takes a few swigs from his glass.

                         DR. NICOLS (CONT'D)
                    (Exhales)
              This show is going to be my last.

                         JO
                    (Surprised)
              What do you mean?

                         DR. NICOLS
              I'm done. I'm tired. I made plenty
              of money on this career, plus my
                         (MORE)

> DR. NICOLS (CONT'D)
> investments turned out well. And I
> want to retire. I'm tired of being
> your teacher and this orchestra's
> idol and inspiration of '*life
> within music*'. I just want a simple
> and exuberant ending and you're
> fucking with it.

Dr. Nicols pours a heavier refill and looks at his glass and
chuckles.

> DR. NICOLS (CONT'D)
> What is surprising about all this,
> beyond these idiots that play here
> and their ass kissing ways. You are
> different. I think... yeah, I think
> that is why I am going to miss you.
> Are you feeling better?

> JO
> A little.

> DR. NICOLS
> (*Smiles*)
> Stand up, won't you.

Jo hesitates on his request.

38   **EXT. CAFE - DAY**   38

At a small cafe / bistro across the street from the
Performance Theater, Bonny and Frankie sit outside enjoying
a cup of coffee and a sandwich.

> FRANKIE
> (*Shocked*)
> Retiring? Are you serious? When did
> he tell you?

> BONNY
> (*Smiles*)
> Last night, in his arms.

> FRANKIE
> (Laughs)
> I bet on the floor of his office.

> BONNY
> You would think so, but that was
> earlier. We did it again, on his
> bed.

FRANKIE
(Shocked)
What about his wife?

BONNY
Away at work. And he's going to
leave her a month after the final
show and we're both going to move
to Montreal.

FRANKIE
When did you all decide on this?

BONNY
Last night.

FRANKIE
That is crazy!

As they sit in silence, Frankie suddenly starts to laugh.

BONNY
(As she takes a bite)
What?

FRANKIE
(Laughs)
Nothing. Well, I was just imagining
about Jo's reaction when she find
out about him leaving. She is so in
love with him.

BONNY
(Disgusted)
I fucking hate her and she is
becoming so annoying with her
sloppy playing.

FRANKIE
At least she makes you look good as
far as stage presence and
performance.

BONNY
I was really hoping he would kick
her out before the show.

FRANKIE
Was he planning to?

BONNY
I tried to convince him. But he
ends up complementing random things
about her instead.

                    FRANKIE
          That's weird.

Bonny sits there reflecting on her last comment. Slowly
realizing that maybe Dr. Nicols preferred Jo over her.

                    BONNY
          Hey, I'll see you inside. I want to
          go talk to Nicols before we start
          rehearsal again.

                    FRANKIE
          Alright, see you.

Standing up, Bonny grabs her purse and starts making her way
across the street towards the Performance Theater.

39   **INT. DR. NICOLS' OFFICE - DAY**   39

Jo nervously stands before Dr. Nicols as he stares at her
with his hungry eyes. Taking another sip, Dr. Nicols rises
from his seat.

Walking around his desk with his drink, he turns on his
stereo and raises the volume as it begins to play classical
music. Dr. Nicols stops at the front of his desk and sits on
the edge.

He takes another swig and finishes his glass. Wiping his
mouth, he places his drink on the table and stares at Jo.

Jo nervously looks up at his face and watches him glare in
lust.

Dr. Nicols slowly rises and walks towards Jo.

40   **INT. PERFORMANCE THEATER, HALLWAY - DAY**   40

Outside Dr. Nicols' office, Bonny smiles as she hears
classical music muffling from his office. She opens the door
but quickly loses her smile as she begins to close the door
to a crack. Just enough to watch Dr. Nicols grab Jo by the
shoulders and rub them. Her eyes begins to look furious.

41   **INT. DR. NICOLS' OFFICE - DAY**   41

Jo becomes very nervous as he starts to massage her
shoulders.

                    DR. NICOLS
          You know, I am very sorry about
          that incident earlier. Do you
          forgive me?

>   JO
>   It's okay, Dr. Nicols.
>
>   DR. NICOLS
>   (Smiles as he combs a strand
>   of Jo's hair her behind her
>   ear)
>   You're very sweet and very
>   beautiful. A talented musician as
>   well.
>
>   JO
>   Thank you.
>
>   DR. NICOLS
>   (Moves his hands from Jo's
>   shoulders down to her arms)
>   Better than Bonny, that's for sure.

Bonny becomes livid after hearing Dr. Nicols' words and
slowly and quietly closes his door.

>   DR. NICOLS (CONT'D)
>   (Comes closer to Jo)
>   Do you have someone special in your
>   life, Jo?
>
>   JO
>   What do you mean?
>
>   DR. NICOLS
>   A man?

Jo stands quiet for a moment.

>   DR. NICOLS (CONT'D)
>   Are you a virgin?

Jo's silence makes him smile. She becomes nervous as she
watches him hold her hands and kiss them.

>   DR. NICOLS (CONT'D)
>   (Observing her hands)
>   Beautiful hands.

Dr. Nicols begins to walk backwards, guiding Jo towards his
desk and to sit on the edge. Reaching for her blouse, he
begins to undo her top button.

Jo quickly reaches for his hands while breathing nervously.

                    JO
What are you doing?

                    DR. NICOLS
Shhh. Don't be afraid. I'll be
gentle.

                    JO
          (Tears begin to form)
Stop.

                    DR. NICOLS
          (Slowly opens Jo's legs and
          pushes up her long skirt)
You and I both know, you want this.

Dr. Nicols quickly leans into kiss her. Jo suddenly becomes
scared and disgusted as he moves from her lips to her cheek
and then her ear. As Dr. Nicols begins to nibble on her
neck, he begins to move his right hand in between her legs,
disappearing under her skirt.

Jo's facial expression changes as she feels his cold hands
move aside her underwear and enter into her vagina. His
fingers slowly reach within.

                    DR. NICOLS (CONT'D)
Oh, yes!

Jo's eyes become watery with fear. Suddenly Dr. Nicols YELPS
in PAIN.

                    DR. NICOLS (CONT'D)
Aaargh!

Dr. Nicols quickly removes his hand and steps back in pain.
He suddenly catches sight of a spider falling from the
darkness between Jo's legs and skirt and onto the floor. Jo
looks down and SCREAMS. She quickly closes her legs and
jumps off his desk.

Covered in black and yellow with a hint of red on its
abdomen. This SCARY looking spider with long, thin legs
quickly scurries away from the scene and disappears under
Dr. Nicols' desk and into the shadows.

Jo finds herself grabbing fistful of her skirt in fear. She
leans against the wall in tears as she quickly looks at Dr.
Nicols.

Dr. Nicols looks at the underside of his right index finger
and sees two puncture marks surrounded by black and purple
flesh. He grabs his hand in pain as he begins to feel
immediately sick and cold sweats appear on his face.

Dr. Nicols suddenly FALLS to his knees as he feels the pain coursing through his arm and then to the rest of his body.

Dr. Nicols FALLS onto his side as Jo slowly slides against the wall towards the door in fear. Jo watches Dr. Nicols struggling to say something as he stares at her with tears sliding down his face and traces of foam bubbling at the corners of his mouth.

> JO
> (Cries out)
> I'm sorry. Sorry.

Jo DASHES out the door as Dr. Nicols shifts his body onto his back as he arches in pain. The SOUND of his heartbeat is heard racing and gradually it begins to slow down. Looking at the ceiling, Dr. Nicols gargles in pain and suddenly exhales his last dying breath.

42   **INT. PERFORMANCE THEATER, HALLWAY - DAY**   42

Jo quickly runs down the hallway way in tears as her shoes echo loudly than ever before.

43   **INT. PERFORMANCE THEATER, STAGE - DAY**   43

Frankie and the rest of the musicians sit idly as they wait for Dr. Nicols to arrive. A musician returns Dr. Nicols' music stand to its place on the podium. Moments later, Bonny appears from backstage with an angry but calm face.

44   **INT. PERFORMANCE THEATER, WOMEN'S BATHROOM - DAY**   44

Jo dashes into the bathroom and quickly enters the last stall in tears. Shutting the door and locking it. She leans against the wall and drops to floor crying.

INTERCUT between WOMEN'S BATHROOM and STAGE.

Bonny makes her way to her seat in stern silence. She looks up to see Frankie's concerned face as she takes a seat.

> FRANKIE
> (Mouthing the words in
> silence)
> Are you okay?

Bonny shakes her head slowly as she exhales her breath like a mad bull.

Jo tries to calm down and slowly rolls up her skirt. She quickly looks scared and covers herself up. Bursting into tears again, she faces towards the roll of toilet of paper beside her and quickly wraps her hand with a small portion of tissue. Jo fearfully wipes her vagina and tosses the blood soaked tissue into the toilet.

MS. BERNARD, a tall and plump woman in her 40's, with red hair in a bob, walks on stage carrying files.

> MS. BERNARD
> *(Looks at her watch)*
> Hello everyone. Where's Dr. Nicols?

Bonny remains quiet.

> PERCUSSION MUSICIAN
> He hasn't come back yet.

Ms. Bernard looks around at the orchestra and notices an empty seat with a violin.

> MS. BERNARD
> Where's Jo?

Jo steps out of the stall and heads towards the sink. Turning on the faucet, she splashes cold water on her face and neck. Grabbing wads of paper towels, she quickly dries her face and tears. Jo looks at her reflection and tries to fix her outfit and hair.

Frankie looks at Bonny's angry eyes.

> FRANKIE
> We haven't seen her either.

> MS. BERNARD
> I see. I'll be right back then.

45 **INT. PERFORMANCE THEATER, HALLWAY - DAY** 45

As Ms. Bernard walks down the hall towards Dr. Nicols' office, she catches sight of Jo stepping out from the bathroom.

> MS. BERNARD
> Jo! Have you seen Dr. Nicols?

Jo nervously shakes her head.

> MS. BERNARD (CONT'D)
> Are you okay? You look sick.

> JO
> *(Nervously nods)*
> Yes, I'm fine. Just a little upset
> stomach.

>   MS. BERNARD
>   Well, you should get back on stage.
>   As soon as I find him, I will let
>   him know you're under the weather.
>   Okay?
>
>   JO
>   Okay. Thank you, Ms. Bernard.

Ms. Bernard continues her way as Jo walks back towards the theater.

46   **INT. PERFORMANCE THEATER, STAGE - DAY**   46

Jo slowly emerges from backstage as she comes up to a quiet orchestra looking at her as she takes her seat. Bonny remains motionless in anger.

Frankie notices the faces of Jo and Bonny and wonders what is going on.

47   **INT. DR. NICOLS' OFFICE - DAY**   47

Ms. Bernard knocks on Dr. Nicols' door and enters.

>   MS. BERNARD
>   Dr. Nicols, the orchestra is...

Ms. Bernard stops with wide eyes. She gasps in HORROR as she sees the director dead on the floor, lifeless with foam sliding down his mouth. She quickly notices his (bitten) hand resting over his chest with fingers outstretched in disfigured form. The skin on his hand and wrist turned black and blue.

Ms. Bernard drops her files and SCREAMS.

48   **INT. PERFORMANCE THEATER, LOBBY - DAY**   48

The lobby is buzzing with musicians asking questions and consoling each others' grief of what has happened. Ms. Bernard sobs as she gives her statement to a POLICE OFFICER.

>   MS. BERNARD
>   I don't know what happened. He was
>   just lying there. Oh God, his
>   face...

PARAMEDICS walk through the crowd towards the exit as they guide a gurney with Mr. Nicols on it, covered by a white sheet and strapped down by black belts.

Jo stands behind the crowd as she catches a glimpse of Mr. Nicols being rolled away. Looking across, she sees Bonny being hugged by a sobbing Frankie. Bonny's eyes were wide with anger and sore red from earlier tears. But the intensity of her eyes are dramatized by the minimal stains of her running mascara.

Suddenly, a man appears in front of Jo with a notepad and a police badge. DETECTIVE WEAVER is a handsome Caucasian man in his late 40's with a scruffy beard and professional haircut.

                    DET. WEAVER
               (Shows his badge)
          Excuse me mam, are you Jo?

                    JO
               (Scared)
          Yes.

                    DET. WEAVER
          My name is Detective Don Weaver. If
          you don't mind, I would like to ask
          you a few questions.

                    JO
          Uh, okay.

                    DET. WEAVER
          First off, I am sorry for your lost
          and I know you want to go home. So,
          I'll try to be briefly as possible.
          Okay?

                    JO
          Okay.

                    DET. WEAVER
               (Flips through his notes)
          When was the last time you saw Dr.
          Nicols alive?

                    JO
          It was during practice, before we
          broke for lunch.

                    DET. WEAVER
               (Writes on his notepad)
          You sure about that? Because I have
          few witnesses say they saw you
          talking to him outside during lunch
          and then following him into the
          building.

                    JO
That's right, sorry. It's just, I
have not been feeling well and
um...

                    DET. WEAVER
Yeah, other people have been
telling me that he was a little
angry with you today? To the point
of throwing his music stand. Can
you tell me why.

                    JO
I was making mistakes during
rehearsal.

                    DET. WEAVER
I see. Did that make you angry? I
mean with him pretty much singling
you out in front of everyone. I bet
you were pretty embarrassed, huh?

                    JO
Yeah, a little.

                    DET. WEAVER
So you made a bunch of mistakes
during rehearsal, he gets mad,
throws a stand, breaks for lunch
and then talks to you outside? What
did you guys talk about?

                    JO
Nothing really. He told me to
follow him.

                    DET. WEAVER
Into his office?

                    JO
          (Silent for a moment)
Yes.

                    DET. WEAVER
What happened next? What did he
say?

                    JO
          (Swallows hard)
He asked if I was feeling well. I
told him 'no' and if I could go
home for the day. I also told him I
would definitely be ready for
tomorrow's performance.

>   DET. WEAVER
>   What did he say?
>
>   JO
>   Well of course he was a little
>   angry, but he said okay and for me
>   to feel better. That was it. Our
>   meeting was short. I left his
>   office and on my way back to the
>   stage, my stomach started hurting.
>   So I went to the bathroom. When I
>   left the bathroom, I saw Ms.
>   Bernard walking in the hallway
>   looking for Dr. Nicols.
>
>   DET. WEAVER
>   And you told her that you last saw
>   him in his office?
>
>   JO
>   Yes.
>
>   DET. WEAVER
>   Well that is strange, because she
>   says you shook your head 'no' when
>   she asked you if you seen him or
>   not?
>
>   JO
>   Again, I wasn't feeling well at
>   that time. I don't remember in
>   exact detail of my conversation
>   with Ms. Bernard.
>
>   DET. WEAVER
>   I see.

Detective Weaver ponders for a moment, then smiles and
reaches into his inside coat pocket to pull out his business
card.

>   DET. WEAVER (CONT'D)
>   (Passes the card to Jo)
>   Well I believe I have everything I
>   need, Jo. So if you think of
>   anything else or remember anything
>   suspicious or odd. Give me a call.
>   Because I will be in touch with
>   you.

Suddenly everyone turns around to the center of the lobby as
Ms. Bernard CLAPS her hands.

>   MS. BERNARD
>   *(Wipes her tears with a*
>   *tissue)*
>   Excuse me, everyone! Excuse me. I
>   just spoke to the board and I
>   understand a lot of you are
>   grieving and heartbroken over the
>   loss of Dr. Nicols. He was the
>   finest and greatest director this
>   institute has ever had. However, a
>   lot of you did not know that the
>   performance tomorrow was supposed
>   to be his announcement for
>   retirement.

The musicians in the lobby gasp and whisper in confusion of this new information

>   MS. BERNARD (CONT'D)
>   Please, stay quiet, because this is
>   very important. In light of this
>   season's performances and of the
>   economy, ticket sales have not been
>   well. And as you all know, we rely
>   on state funding and donors to
>   provide us the opportunity to
>   perform for our community every
>   season. So we cannot afford the
>   risk of canceling tomorrow's event.
>   In the meantime, the Board and I
>   will come together and find a
>   temporary director until one can be
>   filled permanently. I will get in
>   touch with all of you tonight via
>   email for the time of tomorrow's
>   emergency rehearsal. So please, go
>   home and rest and know that if Dr.
>   Nicols were here, he would
>   passionately demand of all of you,
>   that 'the show must go on!'

The musicians stand quiet and knew they had a professional obligation.

49   **INT. JO'S APARTMENT - NIGHT**   49

BEDROOM

Jo cries on her bed until her cellphone laying beside her begins to RING. As she turns to grab it, the screen reads MOM. She answers it.

> JO
> Hello?

50 **INT. JO'S PARENTS' HOME - NIGHT** 50

LIVING ROOM

Jo's Mom stands by a window as she observes the ranch.

> JO'S MOM
> Are you okay? I just saw the news!

INTERCUT between Jo and Jo's Mom

> JO
> Yeah, I am fine.

> JO'S MOM
> I am so sorry sweetie, did you want
> to come home?

> JO
> No, I can't. They want us to
> continue with the show tomorrow.

> JO'S MOM
> I see. But you are doing okay?
> Aren't you?

> JO
> Yeah, I am, don't worry. But I do
> need to ask you something though.

> JO'S MOM
> Sure sweetie, what is it?

Jo sits up from her bed, wiping her tears away and snuffling
her nose.

> JO
> My adoption papers, you still have
> them?

Jo's Mom is silent.

> JO
> Mom? Are you there?

> JO'S MOM (V.O.)
> (Nervous)
> Why do you ask?

                    JO
Do you have them?

                    JO'S MOM
Yes. But you don't need to worry
about all that right now. You need
to get some rest for tomorrow.
Okay?

                    JO
Mom, I need you to send them to me.

                    JO'S MOM
Jo, I - I don't understand why you
would want to trouble yourself with
the past. You are in a good place
right now with your career in music
and might I add, a position with an
excellent orchestra! Why would you
want to ruin all that with
information of terrible things.

                    JO
          (Moves to sit at the edge of
          her bed)
Terrible? Did something terrible
happened to my birth-parents?

Jo's Mom is silent again.

                    JO (V.O.)
Mom?

                    JO'S MOM (V.O.)
          (Breathing heavily and
          sobbing)
Your father made me promise to
never tell you this.

                    JO
Mom, please. Just tell me. I think
we can all agree that I am a grown
up and I can handle what ever
information you tell me.

                    JO'S MOM
          (Wipes away a tear)
Oh, God. Your father is going to
kill me!

                    JO (V.O.)
I need to know.

                    JO'S MOM
          Before we adopted you. We had no
          idea of what had happened to you
          and your birth-mother in that
          forest. The adoption agency lied to
          us.

                    JO
          What do you mean?

                    JO'S MOM
                    (Sobbing)
          Your mother didn't abandoned you.

                    JO
          But, you said she did.

                    JO'S MOM
          I lied. We lied. Your birth-mother
          is dead. As far as your
          birth-father, we don't know what
          happened to him.

                    JO
          How did she die?

Jo's Mom stares aimlessly.

                    JO(V.O.)
          Mom?

                    JO'S MOM
          Well...

                                              BLACK OUT

51   **EXT. AOKIGAHARA FOREST, JAPAN - DAY**   51

TEXT OVER BLACKOUT:

"AOKIGAHARA A.K.A. THE SUICIDE FOREST, LOCATED AT THE BASE
OF MT. FUJI"

Deep within this forest, a SUICIDAL MAN, mid 50's and thin
comes to a small clearing carrying a bottle of Sake with
tears running down his face. Wearing a blue backpack, a
long, guide rope is running through the top opening as it
leaves behind a trail, disappearing into the wilderness
where it is anchored just near a hiking trail. The end piece
of this long rope is tied to the top loop of the backpack.

Suddenly the SUICIDAL MAN feels a tug and he stops. Taking
off his backpack, he notices he was at the end of his rope.

Walking a few feet away from the bag, he DROPS to his knees and takes a few huge gulps of the sake. As soon as he finishes it, he tosses the empty bottle to the side. Breaking down in tears, he pulls out a photo of his wife and children smiling.

He sobs louder as he slowly crumbles the photo in his left hand.

                    SUICIDAL MAN
                 (Speaking in Japanese)
          You fucking bitch! Oh, you fucking
          bitch!

He slowly pulls out a small switch blade.

                    SUICIDAL MAN
               (Looking up and shouting)
          Oh, God! Why would you do this to
          me? Why?

He slowly presses the blade against his left wrist. He closes his eyes, fearing of the pain he is about to inflict on himself.

Suddenly, he hears the SOUND of a CRYING BABY.

He stops the pressure of the blade and opens his eyes.

The crying STOPS.

                    SUICIDAL MAN (CONT'D)
             (He observes his surroundings
              as he wipes away his tears)
          Hello? Is anyone there?

The crying starts again. The Suicidal Man quickly stands up and slowly follows the sound.

                    SUICIDAL MAN (CONT'D)
          Hello? Are you lost? Where are you?

The Suicidal Man TRIPS on a rock and FALLS to the floor. As he lands, he hits his head against a small boulder. Recovering from the pain, he turns his bloodied head and is immediately horrified by the sight before him. The Suicidal Man SCREAMS in terror as he crawls backwards from the scene.

RUNNING back, he passes his backpack and follows the guide rope back into the forest in fear.

HIKING TRAIL

A young Japanese couple, in their mid-20's smile as they hold each other's hands while they hiked the trail. Properly dressed for the hike, they each wore a small backpack.

Suddenly they are surprised by the terrified Suicidal Man running out from the dense forest, screaming.

                    SUICIDAL MAN (CONT'D)
          Help me!

The young HIKER GIRLFRIEND is horrified by the blood on his head and SCREAMS.

HIKER BOYFRIEND stands in front of his girlfriend in defense mode.

Suicidal Man drops to his knees in fear.

                    SUICIDAL MAN (CONT'D)
          Help me!

Hiker Boyfriend kneels by him.

                    HIKER BOYFRIEND
                 (Speaking in Japanese)
          Are you okay? What's wrong?

The Suicidal Man bends down to the soil as he buries his face onto his hands as begins to mumble.

                    SUICIDAL MAN
                 (Mumbling in fear)
          Oh God! I'm sorry, I won't ever do
          it again. I'm Sorry! Forgive me!

Hiker Boyfriend looks to Hiker Girlfriend.

                    HIKER BOYFRIEND
          Call the police!

Hiker Girlfriend removes her backpack and pulls out her cellphone decorated in anime phone charms. She quickly dials as she steps away from the men.

                    HIKER BOYFRIEND (CONT'D)
          What happened out there? Tell me!

The Suicidal Man continues to sob. Hiker Girlfriend finally hears a female POLICE OPERATOR.

                    POLICE OPERATOR (V.O.)
                 (Speaking in Japanese)
          Minamitsuru Police Department, how
          can I help you?

                HIKER GIRLFRIEND
             (Speaking in Japanese)
      Yes, we need help.

                HIKER BOYFRIEND
      You need to tell me what happened!

                SUICIDAL MAN
      It was terrible! Oh God!

                HIKER GIRLFRIEND
      There is man who is hurt, he looks
      like he was lost in the forest.

The Hiker Boyfriend quickly becomes angry by the Suicidal
Man's ranting that he grabs him by the shirt and pulls him
up. Shaking the Suicidal Man by the shoulders, the Hiker
Boyfriend begins to shout.

                HIKER BOYFRIEND
      What happened? What did you see?

                SUICIDAL MAN
      Demons! Demons!

Hiker Girlfriend suddenly stops talking on the phone and
looks to Hiker Boyfriend. Suicidal Man begins to weep in the
Hiker Boyfriend's arms.

              SUICIDAL MAN (CONT'D)
      Demons! They're in the forest! Oh
      God! I'm Sorry!

              POLICE OPERATOR (V.O.)
      Hello? Are you still there? Hello?

LATER THAT DAY

The hiking trail is currently busy with foot traffic of
POLICE OFFICERS and other EMERGENCY OFFICIALS. Suicidal Man,
Hiker Boyfriend & Girlfriend are covered with blankets and
given hot tea.

As Police Officers interview the hikers in the distance,
DETECTIVE HARUKI enters the area. He is in his late 50's and
is slightly chubby with salt and pepper hair. He walks up to
the Suicidal Man sitting on a dead tree, slowly and
nervously sipping his tea as a PARAMEDIC tends to his head
wound.

                DET. HARUKI
             (Speaking in Japanese)

                (MORE)

                    DET. HARUKI (CONT'D)
          I'm Detective Haruki. Tell me what
          happened? What were you doing out
          here?

The Suicidal Man hesitates to look at the detective.

                    SUICIDAL MAN
          I, I just came out here for a walk.

                    DET. HARUKI
          A walk? Your I.D. says that you
          live in Atsugi. Quite a trip to
          come out here just for a walk. You
          stink of sake. You wouldn't be
          trying to do something dangerous
          out here, would you? Something
          dangerous to yourself?

Suicidal Man takes a sip of his tea.

                    SUICIDAL MAN
          Not anymore.

                    DET. HARUKI
          I see. So what happened out there?
          These kids are saying you were
          screaming about demons. What did
          you see?

                    SUICIDAL MAN
          A baby.

                    DET. HARUKI
          Baby? What are you talking about?
          Are you saying there's a baby out
          there? Is it alive?

                    SUICIDAL MAN
          The demon was right next to it.

                    DET. HARUKI
                (Knocks the Suicidal Man's tea
                from his hand)
          Talk to me! Is the baby still
          alive?

                    SUICIDAL
          Just follow the rope.

FOREST

Detective Haruki, TWO POLICE OFFICERS with a trained canine and a FORENSIC MEMBER in white overalls and carrying a large, black case follow the rope trail. Suddenly they hear the sounds of a crying baby.

> DET. HARUKI
> Do you hear that?

The group of men and the canine quickly run towards the sound. As the come upon the Suicidal Man's backpack, they stop to listen. They hear the baby crying again and the dog BARKS.

They dash towards the source of the sound and quickly stop. Suddenly the dog YELPS and runs away from the group and disappears into forest.

> DET. HARUKI (CONT'D)
> Oh God!

The Forensic Member pulls out his camera from the case and nervously raises his camera up and snaps a flash photo.

WHITE OUT WITH HIGH PITCH RINGING FADING

52   **INT. MINAMITSURU HOSPITAL - NIGHT**   52

FADE IN

HALLWAY

This small town hospital is quiet and very few STAFF MEMBERS walk the halls.

MORGUE

Detective Haruki stands before a large window overlooking a small autopsy room. Minamitsuru Medical Examiner - DOCTOR FUMIAKI is an old, frail professional with large thick glasses.

Doctor Fumiaki shakes his head as a middle aged NURSE begins to cover a bulky figure with a large, white sheet. He walks away from the scene as he disposes his gloves and surgical mask in a bio-hazard bin.

Doctor Fumiaki steps out from the autopsy room to meet Detective Haruki. The men greet with a bow.

> DET. HARUKI
> Good evening doctor.

                    DR. FUMIAKI
                 (*Speaking Japanese*)
Good evening detective.

                    DET. HARUKI
What can you tell about the victim.

                    DR. FUMIAKI
Nothing to indicate foul play or
self-harm. The skin itself is dried
out and the organs are like dried
grapes. The victim was a female in
her 30's and the forming of her
hips shows that she was pregnant.
Dry amniotic fluid was found on the
infant and as well on the soil
underneath the victim. Indicating
she delivered the baby a day or two
ago. The clothing she was wearing
and the items found in her hair
indicates she was Geisha.

                    DET. HARUKI
Geisha? Doctor Fumiaki, how did she
end up the way she did?

                    DR. FUMIAKI
That is a good question, detective.
And I don't have an answer. What
ever happened out there, was not
natural. I can't explain it, except
what are own two eyes see. And what
I see and conclude is that those
spiders covered her in layers and
layers of webbing. And from what I
can tell, drank her dry like an
insect caught in a web. And as for
the child, they ran some tests and
found no bites on her or toxins in
her system. She's healthy, perfect
in fact. But the girl's digestive
waste shows traces of spider
remains.

                    DET. HARUKI
What are you saying?

                    DR. FUMIAKI
The spiders fed on the mother and
the child fed on the spiders.

Detective Haruki suddenly feels nauseous.

> DET. HARUKI
> Excuse me doctor.

> DR. FUMIAKI
> I don't blame you detective.

Detective Haruki, disturbed by the information walks away for the nearest exit.

> DR. FUMIAKI (CONT'D)
> (Watches Det. Haruki leave)
> I'll fax you everything I have!
> (Stares at the body and whispers)
> Monstrous!

53 **EXT. MINAMITSURU HOSPITAL - NIGHT**   53

Detective Haruki quickly walks outside and reaches into his coat for his pack of cigarettes. He slips a cigarette in between his lips and tries to look for a lighter as the SOUND of thunder ROARS in the distance. Suddenly he hears an old woman's voice behind him.

> MIKAKO(O.S)
> (Speaking Japanese)
> Crazy day, huh?

MIKAKO, mid 60's with dark hair smokes while leaning against a wall.

> DET. HARUKI
> (Turns towards her)
> No kidding.

> MIKAKO
> (Walks towards him and passes
> him her lighter)
> You the detective who brought in
> that dead woman and her baby?

> DET. HARUKI
> (Takes the lighter and lights
> his cigarette)
> Thanks. What's it to you?

> MIKAKO
> I'm supposed to be looking for you.

> DET. HARUKI
> (Passes back the lighter)
> Yeah?

                    MIKAKO
              (Extends her hand)
         I'm Mikako Takeuchi, I'm with
         social services.

                    DET. HARUKI
              (Surprised, shakes her hand)
         Oh! Yes. I'm...

                    MIKAKO
         Detective Haruki. Yes, I know. I
         talked to the doctors. The kid is
         healthy and I was going to let you
         know that we'll be picking her up
         tomorrow.

                    DET. HARUKI
         What then?

                    MIKAKO
         Well, you know how it is. Once
         officials release the info to the
         news and if no one comes forward to
         claim the child... she goes
         straight into the system.

Detective Haruki exhales the smoke.

                    MIKAKO (CONT'D)
         You alright? What happened out
         there?

                    DET. HARUKI
         Did you see the photos?

                    MIKAKO
         Oh, yes I did. Makes me scared to
         pick up that child. But someone has
         to do it tomorrow and looks like
         it's going to be me. Hey, is it
         true?

                    DET. HARUKI
         About?

                    MIKAKO
         The person who found them, did he
         really kept screaming about demons?

Detective Haruki thought long and hard about her question.

                          DET. HARUKI
              He hasn't stopped.

54   **INT. JO'S APARTMENT - NIGHT**   54

BEDROOM

Jo's sits on the floor in front of her bed, emotionally
drained from what she just heard from her mother.

                          JO
              Wh - why, oh God. Why didn't you
              tell me this before? Why hide this?

                          JO'S MOM (V.O.)
              Jo, try to understand. No one
              wanted you in Japan! I mean NO ONE
              wanted to adopt you after they
              found out about your birth mother.

                          JO
                    (Wipes a tear from her eyes)
              So how did you choose me?

55   **INT. JO'S PARENTS' HOME - NIGHT**   55

LIVING ROOM

INTERCUT BETWEEN JO AND JO'S MOM

                          JO'S MOM
              When I was in college, I was in a a
              car accident. My pelvis area was
              impaled by an iron rod after
              crashing into a fence. I couldn't
              have children. After I met your
              father and got married, he was
              working in corporate finance which
              required him to travel. Japan was
              one of those places. I was in a
              dark place at the time and he knew
              I always wanted children. And
              that's when he saw you. Playing in
              a park with a bunch of other
              orphans. He secretly filed the
              paperwork and surprised me several
              months later with your picture. I
              fell in love and he told me you
              would be mine by Christmas.

                          JO
              Didn't they tell him the truth?

                    JO'S MOM
Of course not honey, he's American.
They took advantage of the
opportunity. And the only reason we
know the truth now is because your
father wanted to know your past,
especially after your fifth
birthday. He hired a private
investigator in Tokyo to find out
as much as he could. After locating
Detective Haruki, he gave up the
files willingly and told the
investigator we hired that we
needed to know the truth about you.
Apparently the case scared him so
much he plummeted towards a life of
smoking and drinking and he was
basically dying at the time. But in
the end he didn't die from smoking
and drinking.

                    JO
What did he die of?

                    JO'S MOM (V.O.)
He committed suicide in the forest.

56   **EXT. AOKIGAHARA FOREST, JAPAN - DAY**   56

Flash scene of Detective Haruki hanging by a self-made
noose. A small spider crawls and scurries out of his mouth.

57   **INT. JO'S PARENTS' HOME - NIGHT**   57

CONTINUE INTERCUT OF JO AND JO'S MOM.

                    JO'S MOM
You know Jo, we do love you and we
will always love you.

                    JO
I need to see these files.

                    JO'S MOM
Fine. I will send you the files
tomorrow. Your father had them
translated after receiving them. So
the transcripts will be in there
too. But just know, the photos are,
well they're just terrible. So Jo,
after you learn everything you
needed to know and if you want to
come home, just come home. Okay?

> JO
> (Sobs)
> I love you mom.

> JO'S MOM (V.O.)
> I love you too, sweetheart.

> JO
> Goodnight.

Jo hangs up the phone and sits silent. Her phone soon jingles of an email alert. Looking at her phone and opening an application, she reads an email from Ms. Bernard that reads:
> "EMERGENCY REHEARSAL AT 10:00 A.M."

58   **INT. CITY MORGUE - NIGHT**   58

Detective Weaver walks into a brightly lit lab where cold, steel gurneys are occupied by corpses. He walks up to DOCTOR VALERIE SCOTT, late 40's and a beautiful African American with glasses and a white coat.

> DET. WEAVER
> Good evening, beautiful!

> DR. SCOTT
> Evening sugar, what brings you
> here?

> DET. WEAVER
> Nicols.

> DR. SCOTT
> Ah, I thought you were here for me.

Detective Weaver smiles and surprises her with a candy bar.

> DET. WEAVER
> I would never forget to bring
> chocolate for a beautiful woman.

> DR. SCOTT
> Rightly so, especially since it is
> my anniversary.

> DET. WEAVER
> Really? And how's Mr. Scott?

> DR. SCOTT
> Good, actually he is on his way to
> pick me up for a late dinner
> celebration. So, you and I are
> going to have to do a quickie!

>   DET. WEAVER
>   You know how I like those!

Suddenly, Rani comes in dressed in a white coat and carrying
a clip board and a jar with an organ soaked in formaldehyde.

>   DR. SCOTT
>   Detective Weaver, I would like you
>   to meet my new, bright and very
>   intelligent intern Dr. Rani Saluja.

>   DET. WEAVER
>   (Shakes her hand)
>   Nice to meet you.

>   RANI
>   Hi! Nice to meet you too. Dr.
>   Scott, Dr. Lee says the results
>   will be ready for you tomorrow
>   morning.

>   DR. SCOTT
>   Wonderful. Dr. Saluja, will you
>   assist me please.

>   RANI
>   Yes, doctor.

The trio walks towards Dr. Nicols' body covered with a blue
blanket.

>   DR. SCOTT
>   Well I hate to disappoint you,
>   detective. But there is no murder
>   case here.

>   DET. WEAVER
>   Seriously? So what happened with
>   this guy?

>   DR. SCOTT
>   Dr. Saluja, would you please.

Rani lifts a portion of the blue blanket to grab Dr. Nicols'
discolored right hand and turns it over to reveal a bite
mark.

>   DR. SCOTT (CONT'D)
>   Nephila clavata.

>   DET. WEAVER
>   Come again?

                    DR. SCOTT
          It's a type of spider. Your victim
          died of a venomous bite.

                    DET. WEAVER
          A spider bite?

                    DR. SCOTT
          Yup, an exotic one at that. Quite
          beautiful actually. All the way
          from Japan. They call it the 'Joro'
          Spider.

Rani pulls out a printout photo of a Joro Spider from her
clipboard and shows it to Detective Weaver.

                    DET. WEAVER
          Interesting.

                    DR. SCOTT
          What is?

                    DET. WEAVER
          The last person who saw him alive
          is Japanese. What else can you tell
          me about this poisonous spider.

                    DR. SCOTT
          Venomous.

                    DET. WEAVER
          What's the difference?

                    DR. SCOTT
          Venomous is for bites & stings.
          Poisonous is for consumption. Just
          imagine the 'v' in venomous as the
          shape of a fang for a spider or
          snake. Anyways, normally the toxin
          of these spiders are of a low risk
          to humans. A bite from these
          certain spiders will turn the wound
          bumpy and red, similar to that of
          an allergic reaction.

                    DET. WEAVER
          Okay. So why is he dead?

                    DR. SCOTT
          Well we did a little digging. Dr.
          Saluja...

Rani removes the entire blue blanket away from Dr. Nicols'
naked body to reveal a horrific scene of a fully discolored
and swollen body. His torso has stitches from an autopsy.

> DET. WEAVER
> *(Shocked)*
> Jesus!

> DR. SCOTT
> His tissue and organs are swimming
> with Joro venom and his nervous
> system are slowly deteriorating as
> we speak. Turning into mush.

> DET. WEAVER
> One bite did this?

> DR. SCOTT
> Normally, it would not. But this is
> not normal. Let alone natural.

> DET. WEAVER
> *(Whispers to himself)*
> No shit.

> DR. SCOTT
> The amount of toxins in his system
> is equivalent to that of the Joro
> spider biting into an insect.

> DET. WEAVER
> We're going to have to shut down
> that theater!

> DR. SCOTT
> *(Chuckles)*
> Good luck with that!

> DET. WEAVER
> What do you mean?

> DR. SCOTT
> Well, I called the theater earlier
> for a request to have that theater
> to shut down. So we can get the
> city to hire a team to go out there
> and do a thorough inspection and
> fumigation. Obviously, this spider
> is dangerous!

> DET. WEAVER
> Obviously. Well what did they say?

                    DR. SCOTT
Well they called the mayor.

                    DET. WEAVER
Oh shit. And?

                    DR. SCOTT
Next thing I know, I get the mayor
calling and screaming at me to keep
this on the down low. Apparently,
he's hosting a special guest from
some Arabic country and they wanted
to see some performance this
weekend, without a 'hitch'.

                    DET. WEAVER
Fucking asshole. So what now?

                    DR. SCOTT
The mayor sent a team of
exterminators to do a quick sweep
of the place tonight and all the
way through tomorrow morning! And
so far they found nothing matching
our spider except a nest or two of
harmless spiders and a few Black
Widows. But they'll keep looking.
And Dr. Saluja sent a sample of the
your guy's tissue to a spider
specialist, so I'm pretty sure
we'll hear something from him soon.
But as far as you're case with
Nicols, it's not homicide.

                    DET. WEAVER
Shit. Well, at least I have my
weekend free now.

Suddenly there is a knock on the door and in enters MR.
SCOTT. A handsome and bald, early 50's African American.

                    MR. SCOTT
Valerie? Oh, sorry I didn't realize
you were with... Oh, hey Don!

                    DET. WEAVER
Charles, how are ya?

                    MR. SCOTT
                (Walks and shakes Det.
                Weaver's hand)
Good, now that I'm here to pick up
my beautiful wife. Are you ready
                    (MORE)

>   MR. SCOTT (CONT'D)
>   sweety? Holy cow, what happened to
>   him?

Doctor Scott quickly covers Dr. Nicols' body.

>   DR. SCOTT
>   *(Kisser her husband)*
>   Oh you know how it is, work - work
>   - work! I'll explain later. Honey,
>   this is my new intern, Doctor Rani
>   Saluja.

>   MR. SCOTT
>   *(Shakes Rani's hand)*
>   Nice to meet you.

>   RANI
>   You as well.

>   DR. SCOTT
>   Well, Detective Weaver - you have a
>   good night.

>   DET. WEAVER
>   You two have a good night as well,
>   happy anniversary by the way.

>   DR. SCOTT & MR. SCOTT
>   Thank you.

>   DR. SCOTT
>   Dr. Saluja will update you if she
>   finds or hears anything new. You
>   good on your own until Dr. Dows
>   comes in for the graveyard shift?

>   RANI
>   Yes, I will be fine. Have a good
>   night doctor.

>   DR. SCOTT
>   You too.

Mr. Scott shakes Detective Weaver's and Rani's hand.

>   MR. SCOTT
>   Goodbye.

Mr. Scott then escorts Dr. Scott away from the morgue. Rani
goes to her desk to grabs some files.

                    DET. WEAVER
              (Observes Dr. Nicols' body)
     I never thought spiders could do
     something like this.

                    RANI
     Freak of nature, if you ask me.
     Then again, nature always finds
     away to bite us on the ass or
     fingers for some.

Detective Weaver walks towards Rani and passes her his
business card.

                    DET. WEAVER
     This is my number, keep me updated.

                    RANI
     Of course.

Detective Weaver makes his way towards the exit.

                    RANI (CONT'D)
     Detective?

                    DET. WEAVER
              (Stops and turns)
     Yes?

                    RANI
     You mentioned a Japanese witness.

                    DET. WEAVER
     Yeah?

                    RANI
     The witness wouldn't happen to be a
     girl named Jo, would it?

                    DET. WEAVER
              (Surprised)
     How do you know her?

                    RANI
     She lives across from me in my
     apartment building and she told me
     she plays at the theater as a
     violinist.

                    DET. WEAVER
     What can you tell me about her?

> RANI
> She's quiet, odd, but she doesn't
> seem dangerous. But, I have only
> known her for a day. I just moved
> into my apartment yesterday. So...

> DET. WEAVER
> I see. Well keep me updated about
> her too?

> RANI
> Oh, okay.

> DET. WEAVER
> Also, this case is between you, Dr.
> Scott and I. Okay?

> RANI
> Oh, no, I understand.
> Confidentiality, I get it.

> DET. WEAVER
> Good. Have a goodnight.

> RANI
> Goodnight detective.

Detective Weaver exits from the morgue as Rani looks at his
card and begins to think.

                                                    FADE OUT

59   **DREAM SEQUENCE - DARK SPACE**   59

Jo has the same terrifying nightmare of the spider woman
engulfed in strobe light. Except this time the light is now
red.

Suddenly a flash image of Dr. Nicols' face covered in blood
appears as the Spider Woman feasts on his neck from behind.

60   **INT. JO'S APARTMENT - DAY**   60

BEDROOM

Alarm clock turns ON and Jo wakes up breathing heavily.

INT. JO'S APARTMENT COMPLEX, HALLWAY - DAY

Jo EXITS from her apartment and locks her door. Rani appears from her apartment and accidentally surprises her.

                    RANI
          Morning Jo.

                    JO
                 (Spooked)
          Oh! Rani! Hey. You scared me.

                    RANI
          Sorry! How have you been feeling?

                    JO
          What do you mean?

                    RANI
          The loss of your director.

                    JO
          How did you...

                    RANI
          I saw him at the morgue and it's on
          the news.

                    JO
          Oh, that's right, you work there.
          I'm okay. I didn't sleep well last
          night. How did he die?

                    RANI
          I'm not on the case. I'm - I'm
          actually working on someone else.
          Do you want to hang out later?

                    JO
          Can't. I have a concert tonight.

                    RANI
          How about after?

                    JO
          Why don't you just come to the
          concert. I have an extra ticket.

                    RANI
          Oh, sure. That would be great.
          Thank you.

INT. JO'S APARTMENT COMPLEX, HALLWAY - DAY

                    JO
Well, I have to go.

                    RANI
Yeah, I have to get ready myself.

                    JO
See you later.

                    RANI
Bye.

Rani watches Jo disappear down the hall and down the stairs.

62   **INT. PERFORMANCE THEATER, REHEARSAL ROOM - DAY**   62

All musicians are sitting quietly in their seats in a small
room. Jo looks to Bonny as she sits and stares at her music
sheet sternly. Ms. Bernard walks and stops before the
orchestra.

                    MS. BERNARD
          Attention, everyone! I know this is
          tough for you all. So I want to say
          thank you all for coming. I am sure
          Dr. Nicols would be very proud of
          you all. We have a lot of things to
          cover. But before we begin, I am
          sure all of you are curious of what
          happened to Dr. Nicols. It has come
          to our attention that he has died
          from a poisonous spider that
          triggered a somewhat allergic
          reaction that sadly turned fatal.

Bonny looks at Jo and back at Ms. Bernard.

                    MS. BERNARD (CONT'D)
          Now, don't worry. The entire
          building has been furiously
          fumigated repeatedly and aired out
          last night and early this morning.
          So we will be practicing in this
          room while the exterminators finish
          the performance hall and lobby. So
          if you see any living or dead
          spiders, please let one of our
          staff know. And do not, I repeat,
          do not attempt to kill it yourself.

Suddenly a door opens and KEVIN enters the room. Kevin is an incredibly handsome, young man, mid-20's with a shaved head and vibrant colored eyes and of mixed ethnicity. Jo, Bonny and all the women and few gay men of the orchestra become immediately attracted to his presence.

> MS. BERNARD (CONT'D)
> *(Smiles)*
> Oh, yes. So the board has found our temporary director. He flew in early this morning from Seattle and he's been incredible in working with us during this unfortunate event. So please help me welcome, Dr. Kevin Bailey.

The orchestra applause.

> KEVIN
> *(Shakes Ms. Bernard's hand)*
> Thank you, Ms. Bernard. And thank you everyone. First off, my condolences in everyone's lost. I didn't have the pleasure of knowing Mr. Nicols personally, but his accomplishments are well known, as well as the success of his wonderful orchestra. So I very much appreciate you all in allowing me to assist in completing the season tonight. We have a lot to cover, but I am confident that we will have a successful performance. So if you all please, I would like to get started now with the first piece.

As Kevin raises his hands, so does everyone's instruments.

> KEVIN
> One, two, three...

63   **EXT. DOWNTOWN PERFORMANCE THEATER - NIGHT**   63

Search lights turn ON and they automatically move as they crisscross their bright beams into the dark sky and across the theater building. Hundreds of elegantly dressed guests walk towards the entrance of the theater, excited of the upcoming performance.

Rani is elegantly dressed in a traditional sari dress with a modern sheen and style.

64   **INT. PERFORMANCE THEATER, WOMEN'S DRESSING ROOMS - NIGHT**   64

In a small room filled with various vanity mirrors, the female musicians prepare as they put on make-up and fix their hair styles.

Jo stands idly by as she watches Frankie and the women do their work. Soon she feels nauseated that she quickly leaves the room.

65   **EXT. DOWNTOWN PERFORMANCE THEATER, BACK ALLEY - NIGHT**   65

Pushing open the door, Jo walks into the cold night, nervously thinking on what is happening to her. As she walks, she quickly notices she is not alone.

She turns to find Bonny in evening wear, smoking under a light with tears in her eyes.

There is an awkward silence between them.

>   BONNY
>   (Exhaling smoke)
>   What do you want?

>   JO
>   I just wanted some air, I didn't
>   think anyone would be out here.

>   BONNY
>   (Walks towards Jo)
>   I understand. It seems like
>   everyone is under stress lately.
>   Want one?

>   JO
>   (Shakes her head)
>   I don't smoke.

>   BONNY
>   (Chuckles)
>   Right. You're a little goody two
>   shoes kind of gal. Huh? But then
>   again, I bet you're the kind of
>   girl that likes to suck Nichols'
>   cock too, huh?

>   JO
>   (Opens the back door)
>   I got to go, show is going to start
>   soon.

Bonny quickly comes towards her and SLAMS the back door shut.

                    BONNY
          I was so wrong about you when we
          first met. What's funny is that, I
          thought you were nothing more than
          a chunk-chink dyke. Boy, was I
          wrong.

                    JO
          I don't know what you're talking
          about.

                    BONNY
          I saw you, bitch! His hands were
          all over you. And you were just
          creaming yourself. I just don't get
          why you killed him.

                    JO
          I didn't kill him.

Suddenly, Bonny GRABS Jo's hair and slams the side of her
head against the door twice and then pulls her down to the
floor.

Bonny quickly POUNCES on Jo and begins to SLAP her endlessly
with ANGER. Jo tries to defend herself.

          BONNY   JO
Don't fuck with me, bitch!   Bonny! Please! Stop! Stop!
You fucking bitch!

          BONNY   JO
He was the love of my life!   Stop!
And you fucking ruined it!

66   **INT. PERFORMANCE THEATER, WOMEN'S DRESSING ROOMS - NIGHT**   66

A knock is heard and Ms. Bernard peeks her head in.

                    MS. BERNARD
          10 minutes ladies. Start making
          your way to the stage!

Frankie puts last minute touches of makeup. A fellow FEMALE
MUSICIAN comes up by her to collect her things.

                    FRANKIE
          Hey, have you seen Bonny?

FEMALE MUSICIAN
No, sorry.

67   **EXT. DOWNTOWN PERFORMANCE THEATER, BACK ALLEY - NIGHT**   67

Bonny and Jo continue to struggle. Bonny's necklace is accidentally ripped off and falls to the floor.

BONNY	JO
I'll kill you! You didn't deserve his fucking attention, you fat fuck!	(Crying) Stop Bonny! Please!

Bonny stops her slapping and quickly grabs fistful of Jo's hair and pulls her face close to hers and screams in fury.

Suddenly Bonny stops her screaming and quickly looks confused and scared. Jo stares up at her with tears and blood from her nose and a scratch on her cheek.

Bonny is horrified to find a BROWN RECLUSE SPIDER crawling out from Jo's hair and up her left hand. The spider BITES!

Bonny SCREAMS!

Bonny quickly swaps it off. Suddenly she notices another one crawling on her right arm. She swaps it off.

Jo's hair begins to ripple in different directions as dozens of brown recluse spiders crawl out.

BONNY
Oh God! Oh God!

Bonny leaps backwards off of Jo and falls on her back as brown recluses begin to crawl on her legs. She begins to scream as she is being bitten all over.

Jo crawls backwards in fear as she combs rigorously through her hair.

Crying for help, Bonny manages to crawl up to her feet and run down towards the end of the alley of passing people and traffic.

Jo notices the remaining spiders disappear into the darkness and quickly tries to chase down Bonny.

JO	BONNY
Bonny! Stop!	(Cries out) Somebody help me! Somebody! Help!

Suddenly a spider bites on to one of Bonny's eyelid. She CRASHES into a couple of pedestrians and wonders blindly and in pain onto the street. Bonny opens her eyes and screams as she becomes engulfed in light. A city bus HITS her and screeches to a halt as her body rolls under the large vehicle.

Jo screams in horror and cover her mouth as pedestrians witness the scene before them and run to Bonny's aid.

Jo watches the event unfold as people scream.

> PEDESTRIAN
> (Screams)
> Someone call 9-1-1!

Jo turns back and runs towards the backdoor of the theater. Making it halfway, she stops and leans against the wall to vomit.

Jo continues moving towards the door and hangs onto the door knob feeling weak and confused. Sobbing, she slowly controls her breathing. She knows there is something wrong with her. She quickly calms down, wipes her tears as she sees the events down the alley become illuminated with flashing red and blue lights from paramedics and police units.

Jo opens the door and notices something glimmering on the ground. Walking towards it, she finds Bonny's Treble Clef necklace. She picks it up and quickly places it in her pocket. Walking back to the door, she opens it again and enters back into the building.

68   **INT. PERFORMANCE THEATER, WOMEN'S DRESSING ROOMS - NIGHT**   68

Jo enters into the empty room and quickly finds her purse. Rushing to a vanity mirror, she looks at herself and is shocked by the blood. She quickly picks up a brush from a near by station and tries fix her hair.

Jo hears a door open and sees Ms. Bernard walking in.

> MS. BERNARD
> Bonny are you in here? Oh Jo, what
> are you doing, show is starting
> five minutes! You need to be on
> that stage right now!

Jo hides her face with her hair as she brushes it furiously.

> JO
> Yes, Ms. Bernard. I will be out
> there in just one minute.

>   MS. BERNARD
> Are you okay?
>
>   JO
>   (Snaps a harsh tone)
> Yes! Just, please Ms. Bernard, just
> give me one minute.
>
>   MS. BERNARD
> This is unacceptable! Please hurry!

Ms. Bernard leaves the room and Jo can hear her talking to
someone.

>   MS. BERNARD (CONT'D)
>   (Loudly)
> Has anyone seen Bonny?

Jo quickly dumps her purse out for the cosmetic back and
wipes her blood off with her sleeve. Finding a tissue box
she pats the blood dry and cleans her nose. She pulls out
foundation makeup, she dabs it over her scratch and blends
it around her cheeks. She quickly looks at herself for final
approval. Jo turns and grabs her music case and quickly
opens it. Pulling out her violin and bow, she rushes out the
door for the stage.

69 **INT. PERFORMANCE THEATER, STAGE - NIGHT**   69

INTERCUT BETWEEN FRONT AND BACK CURTAIN

FRONT CURTAIN

The stage is covered by large red curtains as the audience
fill all the seats. Rani finds her seat close to the stage.

BACK CURTAIN

Jo hurries on stage behind the curtain and notices the
orchestra already in their seats. Kevin stands before them
looking flustered and angry as he quickly notices Jo.

Kevin comes up to Jo angry.

>   KEVIN
>   (Whispers harshly)
> Where have you been?

Suddenly Ms. Bernard appears behind Jo and interrupts.

>   MS. BERNARD
> I can't find Bonny anywhere and we
> can't wait anymore. We have to
> start!

                    KEVIN
          Do what you have to do!

Ms. Bernard quickly walks away.

                    KEVIN (CONT'D)
          This is fucking ridiculous! Take
          your seat Jo!

Jo does as he says.

A follow spotlight is turned ON and Ms. Bernard walks on
stage holding a microphone. The audience applause.

                    MS. BERNARD
          Good evening, everyone! And thank
          you for joining us for our final
          performance of the fall season.

                    FRANKIE
          Dr. Bailey! What about Bonny's solo
          for the finale?

                    MS. BERNARD
          As you all know, we all lost
          someone very important yesterday.
          Dr. Pietro Nicols was not only a
          director to this fine orchestra but
          a great example of what creating
          music can bring to this city.

Rani shifts her head in the mention of Dr. Nicols.

                    KEVIN
          Has *anyone* seen Bonny?

No one answers as Jo remains silent while she stares
nervously at her music sheet.

                    MS. BERNARD
          If you can all join me in a moment
          of silence.

                    FRANKIE
          Dr. Bailey?

                    KEVIN
          We'll have to figure it out during
          intermission. Everyone just get
          ready!

Kevin walks away to the side of the stage and talks to a
random STAGE TECHNICIAN.

                         KEVIN (CONT'D)
           Find Bonny, now!

Stage Technician nods and rushes away.

                         MS. BERNARD
           Our performance this evening could
           not be possible without your
           support. So please, find it in your
           hearts to keep concerts like the
           one you're about to enjoy - alive
           and well in our city! Dr. Nicols
           and his lovely wife, Sheryl would
           greatly appreciate to have his
           legacy and hard work, along with
           his talented orchestra perform not
           only for this night but for many
           nights to come!

The audience applause as Kevin fixes his tie and jacket.
Frankie looks at Jo in anger.

                         MS. BERNARD (CONT'D)
           So without further ado. I would
           like to introduce to you someone
           all the way from Seattle. Who is in
           fact the finest and upcoming
           directors in the nation. Who has
           been named the world's top 100
           directors under 30 and toured as a
           guest director in over a dozen
           countries. And most importantly to
           us, he has been incredibly and I do
           mean incredibly gracious in filling
           in during our unexpected loss of
           not only my friend, but of the
           city's, Dr. Nicols. So please, put
           your hands together for Dr. Kevin
           Bailey.

The audience applause as Kevin walks towards Ms. Bernard.

Ms. Bernard passes him the microphone.

                         KEVIN
           Thank you, Ms. Bernard. And thank
           you ladies and gentlemen. It's a
           pleasure and honor to lead this
           orchestra this evening. And I am
           grateful that the city, the board
           and Mr. Nicols' family and friends
           to allow me a chance to assist in
           finishing their season. So please,
                         (MORE)

> KEVIN (CONT'D)
> do support the arts, the musicians
> you are about to hear and future
> musicians of this city. Who without
> your contribution, cannot do what
> they love to do. Thank you!

The audience applause as Kevin passes back the microphone to
Ms. Bernard.

Kevin turns as the curtains opens to reveal the orchestra,
while Ms. Bernard leaves the stage.

Kevin walks onto the podium, picks up his baton, looks to Jo
and brings his hands up. He gives a down beat and suddenly
the orchestra plays a thematic and intense opening.

As time passes by, Kevin brings a musical piece to a strong
finish, the curtains come to a close and the audiences
applause.

> KEVIN (CONT'D)
> Good job, everyone! Good job! Do
> what you need to do, this is
> intermission!

As the musicians make their way towards the backstage, the
Stage Technician walks towards Kevin, with Frankie standing
close by.

> STAGE TECHNICIAN
> No one has seen her.

> FRANKIE
> I can try to call her again.

> KEVIN
> Do it!

Frankie walks away towards the backstage as Kevin notices Jo
still sitting in her seat.

> KEVIN (CONT'D)
> Jo.

> JO
> Yes?

> KEVIN
> If we don't find Bonny, are you
> able to do her solo?

                         JO
                    (Nervous)
               Uh. Yes. I - I know her solo.

                         KEVIN
               We'll put a stand out for you,
               okay?

                         JO
               Okay. Excuse me.

                         KEVIN
               Of course.

Jo slowly leaves her seat and leaves the stage as she walks
pass Frankie.

                         KEVIN (CONT'D)
               Well?

                         FRANKIE
                    (Shakes her head)
               No answer.

                         KEVIN
               Shit. Someone get me a stand. Jo is
               doing Bonny's solo.

Kevin walks away from the stage. Frankie has a suspicion and
tries to catch up with Jo.

70   **INT. PERFORMANCE THEATER, HALLWAY - NIGHT**   70

Jo makes her way towards the bathroom as Frankie comes up
behind her.

                         FRANKIE
               Hey!

Jo stops and turns. Frankie comes face to face over her.

                         FRANKIE (CONT'D)
               I don't know what the hell is going
               on. But Bonny told me what she saw
               yesterday between you and Dr.
               Nicols doing in his office.

                         JO
                    (Nervous)
               What did she see?

                    FRANKIE
          That you're a fucking slut! You
          completely ruined something special
          between them and now he's dead and
          worst, she has a broken heart.
          She's not here and I'm fucking
          worried. If she did something to
          herself, because of your slutty fat
          ass. I am coming after you.

Frankie quickly turns and walks away.

71   **INT. PERFORMANCE THEATER, WOMEN'S BATHROOM - DAY**   71

Jo enters and rushes to a stall and vomits. Her sickness is
getting worst.

After flushing, she walks towards the sink and turns on the
faucet. As she bends down to wash her face and mouth, her
reflection remains standing with an evil smile. Jo stands
back up to splash her face again. As she looks at her
reflection worrying of what else the night will bring.

Jo suddenly hears something trickling in the drain of the
sink. Is it the spider again?

Jo breathes heavily as she focuses on the darkness deep in
the drain while clenching her fingers on the edge of the
sink. Her breathing suddenly stops as she looks at her
reflection again in anger and then suddenly as if a switch
turned on insider her, her face goes blank.

                    JO
          Bitch!

Jo turns, walks away and leaves the bathroom. Except her
reflection stays and keeps staring forward while the entire
bathroom in the reflection is covered wall to wall and floor
to ceiling with spiders scurrying over each other.

72   **INT. PERFORMANCE THEATER, STAGE - NIGHT**   72

The audience applause as the curtains reopen and the
orchestra plays another furious and thematic piece. Frankie
gives a stern glance at Jo, in which she returns the same
look.

After some time, the moment of Bonny's solo is coming up and
Jo and Kevin knows it. Jo glances to the music stand near
Kevin and she rises and walks towards it.

Rani looks on in excitement and Kevin gestures with support.

Jo raises her violin and begins her solo. It captures the audience in awe as she gradually steps away from the music stand and does her entire segment by memory. Kevin is suddenly amazed and surprised that there is something attractive about Jo.

She finishes her solo, the audience applause as Jo makes her way back to her seat and the orchestra finish their last piece.

Kevin gives a dramatic closing and the entire audience stand in ovation.

> VARIOUS AUDIENCE MEMBERS
> Bravo! Bravo! Bravo!

Kevin and the orchestra give a bow and the curtains close.

73 **INT. PERFORMANCE THEATER, LOBBY - NIGHT** 73

Rani finds Jo in the lobby filled with people and rushes in for a hug.

> RANI
> That was so awesome! I had no idea you were that talented.

> JO
> Thank you!

> RANI
> Oh my God, are you okay? You don't look well!

Kevin suddenly appears with a smile.

> KEVIN
> Excuse me, Jo.

Rani smiles at the sight of him.

> JO
> Dr. Bailey.

> KEVIN
> Can I talk to you for a moment?

> JO
> Of course.

> RANI
> I'll be over here.

                    KEVIN
          Jo, that was amazing! I just wanted
          to say thank you for pulling
          through. I don't know what happened
          with Bonny, but you saved us!

                    JO
          I'm glad it worked out.

                    KEVIN
          It certainly did and because
          tonight was a huge success. The
          board offered me a permanent
          position with the orchestra. So,
          I'll be seeing a lot of you.

                    JO
               (Smiles)
          Wow. Congrats.

                    KEVIN
          Thanks. But keep it between us, no
          one is supposed to know until
          tomorrow. Listen, I was wondering
          did you want to get a cup of coffee
          sometime?

                    JO
          That would be nice.

                    KEVIN
               (Smiles)
          Great, I will give you a call then.
          But hey, I have to get going.
          There's some people I have to talk
          to. Again, great job!

                    JO
          Thanks!

                    KEVIN
          Have a good night, Jo.

                    JO
          Goodnight.

Kevin leaves the area and for a moment looks back at her.

Jo is FALLING IN LOVE!

Rani comes up behind her with a big smile.

>   RANI
>   That is one hot director.

Jo suddenly sees across the room a POLICE OFFICER entering the lobby. Ms. Bernard greets him.

Ms. Bernard nods her head and escorts the Police Officer away from the lobby to talk.

Jo quickly faces Rani.

>   JO
>   I think I should go home now.

>   RANI
>   Okay, I have my car. Come on.

>   JO
>   Thanks.

As Jo and Rani leave the lobby. Frankie observes their exit. Suddenly, Frankie is startled by a weeping Ms. Bernard who is accompanied by a Police Officer and Kevin with a sad face.

>   MS. BERNARD
>   Frankie.

>   FRANKIE
>   Ms. Bernard? What - What's wrong?

74   **INT. JO'S APARTMENT - NIGHT**   74

BATHROOM

Jo stands in the shower motionless as hot steam fills the bathroom.

LIVING ROOM

Jo climbs into bed and covers herself as she meditates of what has happened.

>   FADE OUT

75   **DREAM SEQUENCE - DARK SPACE**   75

A strobe of white light reveals Kevin lying naked on white sheets. He turns his head as a Geisha figure in bright, long, silk robes crawl on all fours towards his body. The woman stops half way over him and begins to ride him.

                         KEVIN
                    (Whispers deeply)
          I love you.

Suddenly, hairy long legs reveal themselves from the robes
and outstretch in all directions over Kevin.

Fast tempo violin music plays a creepy tune is suddenly
heard.

76   **INT. JO'S APARTMENT - DAY**   76

Jo wakes up in terror and tries to shake off the dream. She
rubs her eyes and moves around in bed thinking of Kevin.
Feeling the urge, she begins to feel her way in between her
legs. She rolls her shirt up to show her belly and
underwear. Rolling down her underwear, a small mound of her
pubic bush shows.

                         JO
                    (Whispers as she masturbates)
          Oh, Kevin.

Jo opens her eyes and looks down at her fingers disappearing
among her pubes. Suddenly a hairy TARANTULA camouflaging
itself among her pubic hair flinches over her hand.

Jo SCREAMS in terror as she crawls backwards and hits
herself against the wall and FALLS off the bed.

Freaking out, she looks around her legs, bed and blankets.

Her cell phone RINGS.

Calming herself, she quickly makes her way around the bed
while keeping an eye out for the spider. She answers the
phone.

                         JO (CONT'D)
          Hello?

77   **EXT. CEMETERY - DAY**   77

A large mass of mourners dressed in black break away from a
scene as two coffins are shown decorated with flowers. Large
portraits of Dr. Nicols and Bonny are displayed on easels
with beautiful and expensive wreaths below them.

As Jo walks pass a few gravestones, Detective Weaver appears
with a Styrofoam cup of cheap coffee.

                    DET. WEAVER
          Morning Jo.

                    JO
          Detective Weaver? Morning.

                    DET. WEAVER
          Sorry to hear about your friend.

Jo was surprised by the word, 'friend'.

                    JO
          Bonny was talented.

                    DET. WEAVER
          It's a shame she died just after
          Dr. Nicols.

                    JO
          Yeah. If you're looking for her
          parents, their over...

                    DET. WEAVER
          Actually, I am looking for you.

                    JO
          Oh?

                    DET. WEAVER
          Listen, I would've called but I
          figured you might need a few days
          to... grieve. But we need to talk
          now.

                    JO
          Okay.

                    DET. WEAVER
          Follow me to my car.

The pair walk to his car. Detective Weaver opens the
passenger car and pulls out a sealed plastic bag with the
word "EVIDENCE" on it and filled with a few strands of black
hair.

Detective Weaver passes her the bag.

                    JO
          What is it?

                    DET. WEAVER
          It's hair. Recognize of whose it
          might be?

Jo remains quiet.

> DET. WEAVER (CONT'D)
> The night Bonny died, strands of
> that hair was found on her clothes
> and fingers. Now the medical
> examiner says the official death
> was that bus. But the doc also said
> that she was a victim of spider
> bites from brown recluses.

78   **INT. CITY MORGUE - NIGHT**   78

A flash scene of a naked Bonny, dead on a cold, steel slab.
Blanketed by bright lights over her, a grotesque scene
showing her face, hands, neck, legs and chest with the
horrible aftermath of brown recluse bites: necrotic flesh.

79   **EXT. CEMETERY - DAY**   79

> DET. WEAVER
> Quite a sight, I must say.

> JO
> So why are you showing me this?

> DET. WEAVER
> I've been asking around and it
> seems that Bonny didn't really like
> you very much. So I thought to
> myself. Nicols was mean with you,
> he's dead. Bonny was mean with you,
> she's dead. Then the fact that
> people last saw Nicols alive with
> you and that Bonny and you were
> missing just before the show. A
> pretty blonde with long, black hair
> on her clothes seems strange.
> Doesn't it? So I had to follow my
> gut and come see you.

> JO
> I had nothing to do with their
> deaths.

> DET. WEAVER
> (Chuckles)
> Well, that's why I am here. To sort
> it all out, ask questions, feel
> people out. You know how they do it
> in movies.

Jo stands quiet and nervous as Detective Weaver grabs the
bag from her and puts it back in the car.

>   DET. WEAVER (CONT'D)
>   (Walks around his car)
>   And in the end like all movies, the
>   bad guy or girl gets caught. I will
>   be seeing you again, Jo.

Detective Weaver opens the door, climbs into his car and
drives off.

Jo is suddenly startled by Kevin.

>   KEVIN
>   Jo?

>   JO
>   (Turns around)
>   Dr. Bailey!

>   KEVIN
>   Please, just call me Kevin. I am
>   sorry about your friend.

>   JO
>   We weren't really friends.

>   KEVIN
>   I see. Listen, I noticed you came
>   to the funeral by bus. And since
>   we're both here, I was wondering if
>   you would like to get a cup of
>   coffee with me. And after that, I
>   can drop you off at your place.

>   JO
>   (Smiles)
>   That would be nice.

>   KEVIN
>   (Smiles)
>   My car is this way.

As they walk together, Frankie watches them from the
distance in anger.

80   **INT. DET. WEAVER'S CAR - DAY**   80

While driving, Detective Weaver's phone RINGS. He answers it
while trying to balance his coffee.

>   DET. WEAVER
>   This is Weaver.

                    DR. SCOTT (V.O.)
          It's Scott. I got your results for
          the hair.

                    DET. WEAVER
          And?

81   **INT. CITY MORGUE - DAY**   81

INTERCUT BETWEEN DR. SCOTT AND DET. WEAVER

Rani works on a body in the background as Dr. Scott talks on
her cell phone.

                    DR. SCOTT
          The hair is not human nor animal.

                    DET. WEAVER
          What do you mean?

                    DR. SCOTT
          Well hair is made of a protein
          called keratin. These strands are
          made of silk, very thick silk.
          Almost passes for hair. But it's
          not human.

                    DET. WEAVER
          Silk? Like a spider's web? You
          gotta be shitting me.

                    DR. SCOTT
          There's more. The spider specialist
          says he's never seen or heard about
          these types of attacks, let alone
          the amount of venom we found in
          Nicols. So he's on his way to the
          theater, but we told him none of
          the fumigators found anything
          matching to the spiders that
          attacked the director or the girl.
          There's no trace of them.

                    DET. WEAVER
          Shit.

                    DR. SCOTT
          What do you want me to do?

                    DET. WEAVER
          I don't know. I'll have to get back
          to you.

>   DR. SCOTT
>   Do you still think this is a
>   homicide?
>
>   DET. WEAVER
>   Something is telling me that it is.
>
>   DR. SCOTT (V.O.)
>   Well, you watch yourself honey.
>
>   DET. WEAVER
>   Thanks Doc.

Detective Weaver hangs up and speeds through the traffic.

82   **INT. COFFEE SHOP - DAY**   82

At a small, hipster coffee shop Jo and Kevin sit across from
each other at a small table near a window with large coffee
mugs in front of them.

>   KEVIN
>   So how have you been holding up?
>
>   JO
>   What do you mean?
>
>   KEVIN
>   Bonny and Dr. Nicols.
>
>   JO
>   Honestly, I don't know. I've been
>   confused really. Scared mostly.
>
>   KEVIN
>   Scared?
>
>   JO
>   Yeah. Just strange things have been
>   happening and they are kind of
>   clashing with everything right now.
>   You know?
>
>   KEVIN
>   Not really.
>
>   JO
>   I'm just feeling less... like
>   myself lately.
>
>   KEVIN
>   Well, you're just in mourning.

Jo sits quietly.

                    KEVIN (CONT'D)
          People come out of it eventually.
          Don't you worry.

                    JO
                    (Smiles bleakly)
          That's what I am scared of.

                    KEVIN
          How so?

                    JO
          I am scared that I'll be completely
          changed after all this is done.

                    KEVIN
          Change is good.

Jo wants to scream in disagreement! But remains calm.

                    JO
          So. When do you officially move to
          our city?

                    KEVIN
          Next week. I'll be going back to
          Seattle tonight to get the last of
          my stuff packed and shipped.

                    JO
          Great. Well the orchestra is lucky
          to have you.

                    KEVIN
          I appreciate that. I don't want to
          beat around the bush, but at the
          same time I don't want to
          compromise our professional
          positions. Especially since I'll be
          your new director. You can say 'no'
          and I will understand, believe me.
          But I just need to ask. Would you
          like to have dinner with me next
          Friday night?

Jo simply smiles and gives out a little laugh and nods.

                    JO
          Okay.

                                        FADE OUT

83   **INT. JO'S APARTMENT COMPLEX, LOBBY - DAY**   83

Entering the lobby, Jo walks towards the mailbox area and
opens her box. She pulls out a stack of spam mail and
notices a package from her mother.

84   **INT. JO'S APARTMENT - DAY**   84

LIVING ROOM

As Jo enters her apartment, she quickly drops her stuff and
mail on the couch with the package still in her hands.
Sitting down, she hastily turns over the package and rips
off the seal. Opening the flap, she pulls out the familiar
and old looking file with Japanese characters.

A handwritten note is found paper-clipped on top of the file
with her mother's handwriting. She reads:
    *"No matter what, I will always love
    you! -Mom"*

Jo meditates on the note for a quick moment and sets it
aside. Studying the file, she looks at the condition closely
and opens it.

Papers in English and Japanese, old and new fill the folder.
Clippings of a local Japanese newspaper showing a forest
scene with police officers, the hikers and the suicidal man
in the background.

A manila envelope is found in the middle of the stack and Jo
unravels the string holding the flap.

Jo slowly pulls out the familiar photo slowly and remembers
seeing the top portion. She quickly reveals the rest of the
photo in horror.

                    WHITE OUT WITH AUDIO OF RINGING

85   **EXT. AOKIGAHARA FOREST, JAPAN - DAY**   85

The Forensic Member flashes a photo in horror as Detective
Haruki and the Two Officers witness the scene in disbelief.

                    DET. HARUKI
          Good God!

Before the group of men, a DEAD WOMAN is found leaning
against a tree. The woman's jaw is opened wide while her
face looks up as if she is in pain. Her arms flayed out to
her side and her hair in curls are shuffled with dirt and
leaves. Her colorful kimono is dirtied and ripped. But
overall, the entirety of the woman's body is covered in
spider webs.

Her skin is dried and grey and her eyes sank into their orbital chambers. Her lips curled back in dehydration and her fingers and toes clenched in different directions as she has been stuck in a seizure state.

Between her sprawled feet is INFANT JO. Crying out in tears as she leans against the bony body of her mother.

Various spiders crawled over the dead woman and the infant, while a swarm of them moved about on the trees, on the ground around them and across large walls of webs.

Detective Haruki noticed an instrument beside them, a SHAMISEN. A guitar like instrument, with a long neck and three strings.

Suddenly, the sounds of little spider feet moving stopped.

Detective Haruki and the men noticed it and looked around them for something to happened.

Infant Jo stops crying.

Suddenly the men hears a DROP. Detective Haruki notices something strange. The spiders are simply falling from the trees dead. The spider are curling up and dying.

One by one, the sounds of them falling on the ground sounds like an eerie demonic drum solo. Spiders on the dead woman roll off and the ones on Infant Jo stagger off her skin to their deaths.

Detective Haruki slowly walks towards the infant and carefully tries to not come in contact with the dying spiders.

Taking off his coat, he slowly grabs Infant Jo and wraps her up in warmth. Walking back to the Police Officers, he looks back to face the dead woman again in fear.

                                                    FADE OUT

86   **INT. JO'S APARTMENT - DAY**   86

                                                    FADE IN

LIVING ROOM

Jo looks at the photo of her infant-self next to her dead mother in horror.

Clenching at the photo, she crumbles it up in tears and throws it on the floor. She grabs a page from the stack and crumbles it too. Soon she starts to lose her senses and crumbles, rips, shreds and throws the contents of the folder all around her living room in anger.

Dropping to the floor on her knees, she begins to cry.

                    JO
          Why!? Why!? Oh God, why?

                                        FADE OUT

TEXT ON BLACK SCREEN: ONE WEEK LATER

87   **INT. JO'S APARTMENT COMPLEX, LOBBY - NIGHT**   87

Rani comes in through the lobby wearing her medical scrubs, tired from work as the SOUND of THUNDER is heard in the background. She suddenly catches sight of Jo in formal wear.

                    RANI
          Jo! Hey!

                    JO
          Rani. Hi. You just got off work?

                    RANI
          It's been keeping me crazy busy.
          You look great. Where you off to?

                    JO
          Thank you. I'm actually going out
          on a date. Or at least I think it's
          a date. I hope it's a date.

                    RANI
          It's Friday night, it's definitely
          a date. Where are you all meeting?

Kevin walks in the lobby, nicely dressed in a jacket and tie and carrying a small bouquet of flowers and an umbrella.

                    JO
          He's picking me up.

                    RANI
          Ah.

                    KEVIN
          Hello.

                    JO
Hello. Wow, you look great.

                    KEVIN
You look beautiful! These are for
you.

                    RANI
Those are really nice. Hi, I'm
Rani.

                    KEVIN
          (Shakes Rani's hand)
Kevin.

                    RANI
You're the orchestra's new
director, right?

                    KEVIN
Yes, I am. Nurse?

                    RANI
          (Laughs)
No. Medical Examiner, intern for
now.

                    KEVIN
Wow. I bet you see a lot of messed
up things, huh?

                    RANI
          (Smiles)
You have no idea. Hey, let me take
those flowers for you. You can pick
them up tomorrow morning. I'll keep
them watered.

                    JO
          (Smiles)
Awe, thanks.

                    RANI
You two have fun.

                    KEVIN
It was nice meeting you.

                    RANI
Yeah, you too.

                         JO
              Bye.

Rani watches the pair walk out from the lobby. Kevin opens
his umbrella and they both enter into the rainy night.

88   **INT. JO'S APARTMENT COMPLEX, HALLWAY - NIGHT**   88

As Rani walks up the stairs, she notices Frankie starts
making her way up behind her dressed in jeans and a wet
jacket.

Rani inserts her key into her door and notices Frankie
stopping at Jo's apartment and BANGS loudly on her door.

                         RANI
                    (Turns around)
              Can I help you?

                         FRANKIE
                    (Snaps her tone)
              I'm looking for Jo. Do you know
              her?

                         RANI
              She's not here. Who are you?

                         FRANKIE
              Do you know when she'll be back?

                         RANI
              No. Do you want me to leave a
              message for her?

Frankie huffs in anger.

                         RANI (CONT'D)
              Wait a minute, I recognize you.
              You're in Jo's orchestra, right?
              You play the flute.

Frankie walks away in fury and down the stairs.

                         FRANKIE
              Fuck this.

                         RANI
                    (Talks to herself)
              Holy shit, is every band geek a
              weirdo?

Rani unlocks her door and slams it shut.

89   **INT. RESTAURANT - NIGHT**   89

A fancy, modern style seafood restaurant is decorated in
polished steel and glass with vibrant art and a PIANIST
playing in the background.

Sitting by a window, the glass is covered in droplets of
rain and illuminated by passing traffic. Kevin and Jo are in
the middle of their meal and a funny story.

                    KEVIN
              (Laughs)
          So Charlie did a custom work on his
          French Horn... and every time... he
          gets a break between solos, he
          simply just squeezes the bag in his
          horn... and pretty much just sucks
          up all the whiskey.

Jo laughs.

                    KEVIN (CONT'D)
              (Laughs)
          Oh man, when the show was over! We
          all stood up to bow, but he... oh
          man, did he fall forward, hard!

                    JO
              (Laughs)
          Oh my God! What happened then!

                    KEVIN
          Well people panicked, thinking he
          had a stroke or something. They
          called the ambulance, everyone was
          freaking out. But when they found
          out he had a hangover the next
          morning. Well, they kicked him out
          from the program.

                    JO
          Yikes.

                    KEVIN
          Yeah, but he's cool now. He quit
          drinking, started his own band and
          doing small gigs like teaching
          French Horn to kids. He's happy.

                    JO
          Well that's good.

                    KEVIN
So any crazy stories about you.

                    JO
Me? No! I'm pretty much a boring
person.

                    KEVIN
Pretty, you are. Boring, you are
definitely not! Especially the way
you play.

                    JO
          (Embarrassed)
Thank you.

                    KEVIN
I hope you don't mind me saying
this, but you look a whole lot
better than the last time I saw
you.

                    JO
I feel better.

                    KEVIN
That's good. Anything interesting
that contributed to it?

                    JO
I guess the idea to stop resisting.
Um, the constant challenge of
trying to find the answer and
finally realizing no matter what
happens, I should just let go and
everything will work out
eventually. Even if it's in the
most strange or even scariest of
moments.

                    KEVIN
Kind of like over coming your
demons?

                    JO
More like embracing them.

90   **EXT. RESTAURANT / STREET - NIGHT**   90

Detective Weaver sits in his car down the block from the
restaurant, smoking and drinking his coffee as the rain
drizzles on his windshield. He studies closely of Jo and her
date, talking and laughing.

                                                    FADE OUT

TEXT OVER BLACK SCREEN: ONE MONTH LATER

91   **EXT. CITY PARK - DAY**   91

                                                    FADE IN

Jo and Rani walk at a park on a cold, crisp afternoon
drinking coffee and arms locked with one another. Various
people are seen with their dogs, jogging by themselves or
pushing a baby stroller.

Jo's personality is less depressing and more happier.

                    RANI
          So when do you guys start
          rehearsal?

                    JO
          Next week, Kevin gave me really
          cool solo. So, let's see how that
          goes.

                    RANI
          Nice! He's really smitten with you,
          isn't he?

                    JO
               (Laughs)
          I guess. I don't want to jinx it,
          but I really do like him.

                    RANI
          Did that chick ever get in touch
          with you. The one that plays the
          flute.

                    JO
          Frankie? No. But I did get a letter
          from her sometime after Bonny's
          funeral.

                    RANI
          Really? What did it say?

                    JO
          I don't remember it exactly. I
          burned it. She basically was
          blaming me for Bonny's death.

                    RANI
          Well I hope you're not blaming
          yourself. You know, I didn't want
          to tell you this. But I lied about
          Dr. Nicols. I did have him for a
          case and later assisted with
          Bonny's.

                    JO
               (Scared)
          Why didn't you tell me?

The girls stop and face each other.

                    RANI
          Well, cops got involved honey. And
          I can't talk about a case with
          anyone. At first they thought it
          was homicide, but later conclude
          freak accidents and definitely
          freak of nature when it came to the
          spider bites. But hey...

The girls start walking again.

                    RANI (CONT'D)
          ... at least you got Kevin to keep
          you protected from that crazy
          chick.

                    JO
               (Laughs)
          Frankie is just sad. She lost her
          best friend. But she is a bitch.
          I'm not worried about her. Kevin
          told me last week that she quit.
          So, I won't be seeing her anymore.

                    RANI
          That's good. So tell me about your
          stud! Have you guys done it yet?
          And if so, how big is he?

                    JO
          Well, we haven't done 'it' yet.

                    RANI
What? Jo, my God, that man is so
sexy. The first time I saw him, I
wanted to fuck him right in front
of everyone in that lobby.

                    JO
          (Laughs)
He's actually quite a gentleman.

                    RANI
You're a virgin, huh?

Jo stops.

                    JO
I'm scared.

                    RANI
          (Hugs Jo)
Oh honey, don't be! It's always
scary for the first time.

                    JO
I'm not sure if I'm going to be
good at it.

                    RANI
Does he know?

                    JO
Yeah, in fact he wants to make it
special when we finally do, do it.

                    RANI
What do you mean?

                    JO
He wants me to go on a weekend trip
with him at a cabin he rented.

                    RANI
          (Jumps and screams in
          excitement)
Oh my God, girl! You know what this
means?

                    JO
No. What?

                    RANI
We need to get you some fucking
lingerie! Come on, I know a place.
                    (MORE)

RANI (CONT'D)
This is going to be fun! I promise
you!

Jo and Rani laugh as the walk.

92   **INT. JO'S APARTMENT - DAY**   92

BEDROOM

Jo is packing her bag with clothes while classical music is
playing from her stereo. She lifts up a sexy, black lace
corset and laughs. She folds it carefully and places it in
her bag.

LIVING ROOM

Jo's front doorknob is jiggling and slowly the door opens.
Frankie slips into the apartment like a stealthy cat while
wearing black gloves.

As she creeps closer to the music, Frankie places her key
picking tools in her small black bulky bag and notices Jo.

BEDROOM

As Jo continues her packing, she is suddenly STRUCK with
something blunt from behind and falls to the floor
unconscious.

               BLUR OUT TO BLACK WITH HIGH PITCH RINGING AUDIO

KITCHEN

                                                    FADE IN

                    FRANKIE (O.S.)
          Where is it?

Jo slowly wakes up tied to a chair with classical music
still playing from her room. Her mouth gagged and hands
bound with rope from behind and her legs to the legs of the
chair near the dining table. She hears Frankie walking
around her apartment, searching through her things and
making a mess of the entire apartment.

                    FRANKIE (O.S.)
          Where is it!?

LIVING ROOM

Digging furiously through Jo's property. She finally finds
Bonny's Treble Clef necklace on the floor among the stuff
she threw earlier. Frankie walks slowly into the Kitchen
furious and removes Jo's gag.

> FRANKIE
> I told you bitch. Oh, I told you I
> would be after your fat ass.

> JO
> How did you get in?

> FRANKIE
> You would be surprised what you can
> buy on Amazon and learn on YouTube.

> JO
> Frankie. You need to stop. I didn't
> do anything to Bonny.

> FRANKIE
> Shut up! They said it was a freak
> accident. And I knew in my heart
> that it wasn't.

Jo starts to tear up a bit as Frankie sits in a chair across
from her.

> FRANKIE (CONT'D)
> (Taping on her head/temple)
> But I kept thinking and thinking
> that what happened to her had to be
> done by you. You were always the
> quiet freak. I knew there was
> something off about you.

> JO
> (Cries)
> Please!

> FRANKIE
> (Looks at the necklace)
> I gave this to her as a birthday
> gift last year. I so loved her. I
> mean, I really loved her. She
> didn't know it but I didn't want to
> mess things up between she and I.
> You know? But when I found out
> about her and Dr. Nicols. What
> could I do? What could I say?

Jo tries to fidget her hands but it was no use.

                    FRANKIE (CONT'D)
As Dr. Nicols was very popular, I
couldn't blame her. But I can't
deny the fact I was a little happy
when I found out he died. But that
completely went the other way when
I found out about Bonny. The day of
her funeral, I asked her parents if
Bonny was buried with the necklace
I gave her and they said 'no'. In
fact, they haven't seen it since
they packed up her apartment. Lucky
for me, it just takes a bottle of
whiskey and a hand job for an ugly
police officer to get me a copy of
her file. Police report mentioned
nothing of a necklace among her
personal belongings that night. And
that's when I knew it was taken.
She never goes anywhere without it.
Why did you do it?

                    JO
I didn't kill her.

                    FRANKIE
          (Slams her hand on the table)
Stop lying! Just stop! Because it's
not going to make any difference
now.

Frankie stands from her seat and heads to a drawer and pulls
it open and grabs a large knife.

                    JO
Frankie! Don't do this! Stop!

Frankie walks towards Jo and gags her. Standing behind her,
she tips Jo back and drags the chair to her bedroom while Jo
strains to scream.

BEDROOM

Dragging Jo into the dim room, Frankie pushes Jo's seat
forward.

                    FRANKIE
You my dear, are going to commit
suicide. Looking at you, no one
would be surprised.

Frankie looks around Jo's apartment for something to write.
She finds her music sheets and a red marker.

                    FRANKIE (CONT'D)
                   (As she writes)
              'I killed Bonny. I can't take it
              anymore! -Jo'

Frankie takes the music sheet and presses it against Jo's
hand. Placing the sheet on the table, Frankie sits on the
bed. She looks at Jo for a moment and then removes the gag.
Frankie crosses her legs while placing the knife beside her.

                    FRANKIE (CONT'D)
              I got the prints, now I just need
              the body. Any last words?

                    JO
              No one is going to believe I wrote
              that.

In the darkness underneath Jo's bed, three spiders crawl
their way towards Frankie's leg.

                    FRANKIE
              Have you not seen yourself? I'm
              pretty much doing you a favor. Come
              on, you're not that pretty and it
              shocks me to know that Dr. Bailey
              has the hots for you. I am starting
              to think he has a small dick and
              he's too scared to get a real
              woman.

                    JO
              You don't have to do this.

                    FRANKIE
              Bonny would've wanted me to. You
              know what would make you more
              pathetic in the newspapers. You
              being found dead with bad makeup
              on. Where's your bag?

Jo remains silent.

                    FRANKIE (CONT'D)
              I bet it's in the bathroom. No
              worries, I'll get it.

Frankie uncrosses her legs, gags Jo again, stands up and
forgets her knife on the bed.

She takes the first step and Frankie suddenly TRIPS forward.
Her face SLAMS onto the floor, busting her front teeth.
Frankie SPITS a bloody tooth out in pain.

Jo is shocked to see Frankie's foot covered in webbing with a trail disappearing underneath the bed. Frankie slowly looks back to see what her foot was caught on.

Suddenly, Frankie feels a pull. She SCREAMS as she is dragged underneath Jo's bed, scratching the floors as she disappears into the darkness. The screams STOP!

Jo breathes heavily in fear. After a few moments, she gains control of her breathing and looks around in tears. She notices the knife and slowly tries to scooch towards it. Coming close enough, she struggles as tries to turn her chair around and scooches backwards. Feeling her hands by the bed, she pulls at the sheets towards her until she is able to feel the knife.

Taking hold of the knife, she carefully maneuvers the blade towards the rope. Slowly but surely, she is cutting through.

Finally freeing her hands, she cuts the rope from her legs. Jumping off her chair, she looks at the space underneath the bed in fear. She quickly turns OFF her radio.

Jo's cell phone suddenly RINGS and she screams.

Jo notices her phone on the night stand by her bed and walks towards it. The screen reads KEVIN.

She answers it.

                    JO
          (Wiping away her tears)
     Hello?

                    KEVIN (V.O.)
     Hey, I'll be there in five minutes.

                    JO
     What? Oh! Take your time, I'll be
     waiting.

Jo hangs up and quickly grabs her bag and zips it close. She looks at her bed in fear as she makes her way to the bathroom.

BATHROOM

Jo grabs the last of her things and notices her disheveled look. She quickly washes her face and combs her hair and removes the gag.

She pulls out a Band-Aid and quickly places it on the small opened wound on the back of her head.

LIVING ROOM

Jo notices her apartment is in a complete mess.

>   JO (CONT'D)
>   Oh God!

Suddenly, a KNOCK.

>   JO (CONT'D)
>   (Shouts)
>   I'm almost ready.

Jo goes THROUGHOUT her entire apartment, to turn anything electrical off. Closing all the blinds, anything to make the apartment dark.

93   **INT. JO'S APARTMENT COMPLEX, HALLWAY - DAY**   93

Kevin is waiting at the door in rugged clothing and suddenly hears the door open.

Jo dashes out and quickly closes the door to lock it.

>   KEVIN
>   Whoa! Where's the fire?

>   JO
>   Oh! Sorry.

Jo turns around with a smile and quickly kisses him on the cheek.

>   JO (CONT'D)
>   I'm just excited. Let's go!

>   KEVIN
>   Here, let me help with your bag.

Jo passes her bag and grabs onto Kevin's arm. She escorts him hastily away from apartment.

>   KEVIN (CONT'D)
>   Whoa! Slow down.

94   **INT. KEVIN'S JEEP - DAY**   94

Jo watches the traffic pass by and soon skyscrapers turn into woods.

95   **EXT. CABIN - DAY**   95

Kevin and Jo drive up to a small and simple wooden cabin in the middle of the woods, far from the city.

                    KEVIN
          What do you think?

                    JO
          Wow. It's really nice.

                    KEVIN
          Come on, let's check the place out.

96   **INT. CABIN - DAY**   96

LIVING ROOM

Kevin and Jo enter the cabin minimally decorated with wooden furniture and a fireplace.

Kevin comes up behind Jo, hugs and kisses her on the cheek.

                    KEVIN
          What do you think?

                    JO
          It's really nice.

                    KEVIN
          What's wrong?

                    JO
          Nothing.

                    KEVIN
          Come on, tell me.

                    JO
          Just a lot of things are happening
          right now.

Kevin turns Jo around.

                    KEVIN
          Well, if you're worried about all
          the bad things that happened, it's
          all in the past.

                    JO
          It's just... I am still figuring
          things out. And for some reason,
          bad things are still happening to
          me. And I'm scared that you'll...

> KEVIN
What?

> JO
Well, look at you. You're
incredibly handsome and look at me.
I keep wondering how and why you
would take an interest in me.

> KEVIN
Honestly? I didn't really notice
you until your solo. The way you
played and how you looked and you
somehow made that scared little
girl disappear and replaced it with
something to behold. And I knew I
had to know you.

Jo felt moved and even more so when Kevin gives her a pop
kiss.

> KEVIN (CONT'D)
This weekend is going to be special
okay. So explore the cabin, I'll be
right back. I'm going to get our
bags and the groceries.

> JO
Okay.

Kevin leaves the cabin.

As Jo explores the INTERIOR, she periodically looks out the
window to see if she can catch sight of anything
interesting.

BEDROOM

As Jo comes to a small bedroom with a big, fluffy bed she
notices a gift with a big, red bow. It's a violin case made
of the finest black leather with gold tone clasps. She walks
towards it with a nervous smile. She slowly opens the case
to find a brand new and beautiful black varnished violin and
bow with gold tone strings and bow-hair.

> KEVIN (O.S.)
You know you deserve the best.

> JO
> *(Turns around)*
It's beautiful. I don't know what
to say.

Kevin walks towards her and they engage in a kiss. Jo feels like this is the moment as they passionately prolong the kiss. Suddenly Kevin stops.

> KEVIN
> I don't want to rush it. Let's wait till tonight, I want it to be completely perfect for you. I'm going to go chop some wood and get the fire place started and then dinner.

> JO
> Okay.

Kevin and Jo kiss one more time. They stop and Kevin walks away from the bedroom. Jo looks at the violin and touches it softly.

FADE OUT

97   **INT. CABIN - NIGHT**   97

FADE IN

LIVING ROOM

Sitting on the floor with some pillows and a blanket in front of the fireplace. Jo sets aside her dinner plate as her new violin case sits opened beside her. Jo looks at the instrument as if hypnotized. She is surprised as Kevin appears beside her with two glasses of red wine. As he passes one to her, he sits next to her.

Kevin studies her as she studies the details of the violin.

> KEVIN
> You okay?

> JO
> I don't deserve this. It's...

> KEVIN
> Stop. I know we've only been seeing each other for about a month. But something about you is alluring. And I can't let that go. Hearing you play is hauntingly attractive, if I can put it delicately.

> JO
> You make me sound dangerous.

> KEVIN
> Maybe I like that. And maybe I can
> see that you have an incredible
> talent that can take you all around
> the world. You know, we would make
> a great team.

> JO
> (Looks at Kevin)
> I am just scared of everything
> right now.

Kevin combs her hair around her ear, pulls her in and kisses
her.

> KEVIN
> You don't have to be scared. I'm
> right here and I'm not going
> anywhere. I get it that your
> different and I like that.

Jo loses herself in his words and kisses him. They both
become insanely passionate. They begin to undress each
other. Kevin kisses her everywhere and they soon find each
other naked in missionary form as the wood CRACKLE in the
fireplace.

Kevin and Jo simultaneously ORGASMS.

FADE OUT

98   **DREAM SEQUENCE - WHITE SPACE**   98

FADE IN

A Geisha (her birth-mother) in a gorgeous kimono bows down
and up and then smiles. She is carrying her Shamisen and
begins to play a traditional piece while her eyes are
closed. As she plays, her fingertips begin to bleed and
various spiders begin to appear and scurry in all direction
from beneath her long, flowing kimono. Suddenly she cocks
her head and opens her eyes to reveal scary, demonic RED
EYES.

99   **INT. CABIN - NIGHT**   99

LIVING ROOM

A tarantula quickly scurries pass Jo sleeping (on her side)
on the floor without being noticed as she wakes up from a
nightmare.

Jo is spooked by the crackling of the fire and looks at the flames. She notices Kevin is not lying next to her. She rests her head for a bit and tries to shake off the nightmare. She turns on to her back and is quickly HORRIFIED.

On the ceiling, Kevin is OUTSTRETCHED and covered in webbing as various spiders scurry all over him. A portion of his face shows him with a frightful expression and his hand reaching out for her.

Jo SCREAMS.

A spider pounces from the ceiling onto Jo. She scurries away as she tries to cover herself with the blanket as more and more spiders begin to appear from various hiding spots in the cabin. She screams as she escapes through the front door.

100   **EXT. CABIN - NIGHT**   100

Jo runs to the Jeep only to discover it covered in webbing and more spiders. She runs into the woods, illuminated by full moon.

101   **EXT. WOODS - NIGHT**   101

Jo finds herself exhausted and cold. Suddenly she feels a pain in her stomach and stops. She falls to the floor and struggles in pain. Spiders start to appear in all directions and climb over her. She swaps them off in terror as they slowly wrap her up in webbing.

Jo starts to be tugged to a nearby tree as she screams for help. Soon she finds herself wrapped in what was becoming a large cocoon. Being hoisted up in the air, her loose arm starts to wiggle for something to grab on.

VIEW OF WOODS HORIZON AND FULL MOON

Jo screams.

                                                          BLACK OUT

102   **EXT. WOODS - DAY**   102

                                                          FADE IN

The woods are quiet and the sun is slowly rising. All the spiders in the woods and among the trees and the cocoon begin to slowly die off. Suddenly, the cocoon grumbles and shakes.

103   **INT. JO'S APARTMENT COMPLEX, LOBBY - DAY**   103

Rani pulls out her mail from the box while dressed in her medical scrubs and coat. She quickly notices Detective Weaver walking in.

                    RANI
          Detective Weaver?

                    DET. WEAVER
          Oh, morning.

                    RANI
          Morning. What are you doing here?

                    DET. WEAVER
          I'm looking for Jo.

                    RANI
          Sorry to tell you, she's gone for
          the weekend.

                    DET. WEAVER
          Damn it. Did you just get off work?

                    RANI
          Yeah. So, what do you need with Jo?

                    DET. WEAVER
          I need to talk to Jo about a girl
          named Frankie.

                    RANI
          The orchestra chick? The one that
          plays the flute?

                    DET. WEAVER
          Yeah. When was the last time you
          saw her?

                    RANI
          She was here about a month ago with
          an attitude looking for Jo.

                    DET. WEAVER
          Yeah. Frankie's roommate explained
          that she really dislikes Jo,
          especially after Bonny's death.

                    RANI
          Oh. Well is Frankie okay?

> DET. WEAVER
> Well that's why I am here. Her
> roommate says she hasn't seen or
> heard from her since yesterday. And
> with two orchestra members dead, I
> figured I would look into it.

> RANI
> I see.

> DET. WEAVER
> I know you're her friend and all.
> But I need you to answer some
> questions about her, in detail.

> RANI
> I understand. Come on up, I'll make
> you some coffee.

104   **INT. JO'S APARTMENT COMPLEX, STAIRS AND HALLWAY - DAY**   104

Rani and Detective Weaver walk up the stairs.

> DET. WEAVER
> So I did some more research on that
> Joro spider.

> RANI
> Yeah and what did you find?

> DET. WEAVER
> Turns out it was named after a
> certain 'Yokai'.

> RANI
> Yokai?

Rani and Detective Weaver turn into the hallway.

> DET. WEAVER
> Their types of Japanese spirits or
> demons. The spider that bit Nicols
> was named after what the Japanese
> call, Jorogumo.

The pair stop at Rani's door.

> RANI
> (Puts her door key in)
> Jo-ro-gumo. That's interesting.

Detective Weaver suddenly takes a whiff of something putrid
in the air. He turns around and stares at Jo's door.

>   DET. WEAVER
> Do you smell that?

>   RANI
>   (Stops and smells the air)
> Yeah. Smells like work.

>   DET. WEAVER
> Like your clients at a morgue?

>   RANI
>   (Turns and face Jo's door)
> Yeah. That's Jo's place.

>   DET. WEAVER
>   (Knocks on Jo's door hard)
> Jo? Are you there? This is
> Detective Weaver. Please open the
> door.

He knocks again.

>   DET. WEAVER (CONT'D)
> Did you see Jo leave for the
> weekend?

>   RANI
> No.

>   DET. WEAVER
> Well, someone is in there?

Detective Weaver tries to open the door, but it's locked. He
quickly pulls out a gun.

>   DET. WEAVER (CONT'D)
> Step aside and stay here.

Rani moves away as Detective Weaver pulls out his gun and
suddenly kicks open the door.

105   **EXT. WOODS - DAY**   105

The cocoon begins to rock from side to side, as the
grumbling noises being to grow louder as something is moving
within.

107   **INT. FRENCH CONCERT HALL - NIGHT**   107

FADE IN WITH CONTINUOUS SOUND OF APPLAUSE AND CHEERS

The concert hall is luxurious and refine with an adoring
audience standing in ovation at a stage occupied by a very
large orchestra. The incredible view behind them is of Paris
and the Eiffel Tower at night.

Appearing on stage is the ever beautiful Jo. She is dressed
in a long and silky, flowing dress with bright hues of
yellow, black and a hint of red. Just like the Joro Spider.
Her hair is shiny with loose curls and decorated with an
exotic hair comb in the shape of an arachnid. She walks to
the center stage with her black and gold violin that Kevin
gave her.

> ANNOUNCER (V.O.)
> *(Speaks in French)*
> Ladies and Gentlemen, please
> welcome our special guest:
> Mademoiselle Jo.

Standing front and center with her bare back shown to the
orchestra. Jo lifts her shiny violin and bow as the audience
quiets down.

She begins her solo with a long and eerie note.

BLACK OUT

FADE IN TEXT: **THE END.**